CAREER
OPPORTUNITIES
IN RELIGION

CAREER
OPPORTUNITIES
IN RELIGION

A Guide for Lay Christians

WILLIAM H. GENTZ

HAWTHORN BOOKS, INC.
Publishers/NEW YORK
A Howard & Wyndham Company

Library of Congress Catalog Card Number: 79-84206

ISBN: 0-8015-3200-0

1 2 3 4 5 6 7 8 9 10

Contents

v

Contents

Introduction

Where will you be in A.D. 2000?

That is a question many people are asking themselves or others as we approach the end of the twentieth century.

It is a question that implies a decision about one's career—what one does to make a living. Any thinking person wants to have a career that is not only interesting and challenging but also makes some positive contribution to the world in which we live.

Thus many people are asking the question: "Is there a career for me in religion?"

This book is written to answer that question with a resounding Yes!

The next questions very often asked are: "Does this mean that I must be ordained?" "Aren't careers in religion mostly for the clergy?"

This book answers those questions with a resounding No!

It is the purpose of the book to provide information about occupations in religion for the unordained Christian. It will be of help to young people who are involved in an initial decision-making process. It can also be of help to those in mid-career who are wondering whether there are careers for them too, that match their commitment to the Christian cause.

This book is also a tool for those involved in helping others in career planning: clergy, education directors, and counselors in the local church or denominational office as well as counselors in the public school or college setting.

To those seeking to know what is available in careers in religion, this book offers information about training and experience needed and where to find more sources of help in the career-planning procedure. Occupations are listed at all levels in the churches—the local congregation, the denomination's headquarters or regional locations and institutions, interchurch and ecumenical organizations. There is also a survey of the growing number of possibilities for occupation in non–church-related organizations in the United States and throughout the world. To those who may have the impression that the day of world missions is over, this book points out that it is just beginning. It is a different kind of mission work than was done in the past, but the international opportunities are much greater and the fields are much larger.

We realize also that a career in religion is something very personal, requiring a dedication to the cause of the career that is possibly more intense than that required in other occupations. Thus one of the major purposes of this book is to get readers in touch not only with the opportunities that are available but also with the people who can help them analyze themselves and their motives and see how they fit the positions that are waiting to be filled. The word "vocation" is used a great deal in religious circles to describe a religious career. The root of this word suggests that a religious vocation is a "calling"—that is, the person is responding to a voice to fulfill a life's destiny. Because there are so many theological differences among Christians, we won't attempt in this book to define this "call" too specifically, but the idea of a calling is a common thread running through all religious life, and one that the person thinking about a career should consider. Religious careers are not for everyone; that fact is obvious. But for those who are devoted to the Christian cause and are looking for a life work that corresponds to this, a religious career will be most satisfying.

Because the field is so wide and so diverse, it is difficult to find the careers that are available, but this book will aid in the joyous discovery that there are thousands of opportunities ready and that religious careers are expanding in our world faster than there are persons to fill them. Each chapter of this book surveys an area of opportunities. But it is only a surface survey— there is much more to be found and this book will serve as a map to help the reader find the way to the careers that are there. It is hoped that it will also inspire readers to search creatively for a career to match the goals that they have for their lives.

CAREER OPPORTUNITIES IN RELIGION

1

Careers in the Local Church

To the person looking toward a career in religion the logical place to begin is the local church, where the vast majority of religious careers are available. It is interesting to note that the majority of these careers were unheard of fifty or more years ago. Before that time, the only paid employee of the local church was the clergyman, and often his services were part time in the smaller churches, where he was given a "parsonage" or "manse" with a few adjoining acres of land which he could plant with crops to provide for his family, and have the cow or two and the chickens needed to make ends meet.

But all of that is changed now. In the most rural areas of our country one finds churches with multiple staffs—many of them composed of unordained people who have special skills and training which can be used by the church and which make it possible for them to have "religious careers."

1

In this chapter we will deal in some detail with eight of the major church careers available to the unordained, and we mention some others and various combinations. At the end of this chapter we have included some sample job descriptions from representative large churches. (See also the total list in Appendix A.) These show the wide range of church occupations available today. The variety is surprising and encouraging to the person looking for a career in the local church.

EDUCATION DIRECTOR

The education director in a local church may be designated by a variety of titles. Perhaps the most common is Director of Religious Education (DRE), although some churches prefer to use Director of Christian Education (DCE). In Catholic churches this person is often called the Parish Coordinator of Education, a comprehensive title that describes the position well. In some churches the preferred title is Minister of Education since the title "minister" no longer refers only to the ordained. Whatever he or she is called, the education director is charged with the supervision of the whole educational program of the local church.

Responsibilities

The various responsibilities involved in this position are as follows:

• Serves as advisor to the Committee on Christian Education of the congregation

• Carries out the plans and policies formulated by the Committee on Christian Education
• Formulates class schedules and maintains class records for all schools of the congregation
• Recruits teachers and other leaders for the congregation's education program
• Gives guidance and advice on lesson planning and teaching techniques to teachers in the schools of the congregation
• Plans teacher institutes for the orientation of new teachers
• Directs programs for the upgrading of teaching skills
• Serves as consultant and resource person to the congregation's organizations
• Coordinates the education program with the plans of other committees of the congregation
• Interprets the theology and philosophy of the church's plan for parish education to committees, auxiliaries, the teaching staff, and the congregation
• Serves as counselor and guide to all personnel who are under the direction of the Committee on Christian Education
• Visits the homes of the members of the congregation to acquaint them with the needs and goals of the education program and to encourage them to participate in the total life of the congregation
• Conducts periodic review and evaluation of the congregation's total education program
• Develops a program budget
• Acts as the congregation's representative to the community, district, the judicatory body of the church, and interchurch agencies, in education concerns

A good summary of what the education director is expected to do is spelled out by Louise McComb in these five rhyming words: [1]

- *Analyze* the program of education in the church—through observation, interviews with the clergy, teachers, and board members.
- *Organize* by making plans for general and specific goals.
- *Supervise* others from the wings rather than at the center of the action.
- *Deputize* others to carry out the total program.
- *Synchronize* his or her work with that of all others on the staff and in the program of the church. The ministry is a team, with everyone involved in some type of education in the church.

All this sounds complicated, and it is. The work of an education director involves many different facets of the church's program and means working with many different people and on several projects at the same time. This is described by Louise McComb at the beginning of her book when she answers the question, "DCE—What's that?" with these words:

"The director of Christian education, seen through the congregational periscope, is many things to many people. To the parents of a tenth grader, he may be the adult who is "good with young people" and . . . has their son's confidence. . . . To the tenth grader himself,

[1] Louise McComb, *DCE: A Challenging Career in Christian Education* (Atlanta: John Knox Press, 1963), pp. 34–41.

the director may be the adult who gives him the boost his self-confidence needs. . . . To a kindergarten child, he may be the . . . friend who . . . is genuinely interested in knowing that he has a new puppy. To the kindergartner's teacher, he may be the person who can give practical help in teaching techniques, who bolsters her morale when she is discouraged. To a church officer, he may be . . . well-informed . . . with just the vision the church needs, or he may seem a . . . youngster whose progressive ideas need careful watching. To his contemporaries, he may be . . . someone wasting his . . . talents . . . or one whose life demonstrates the happiness to be found in a . . . church vocation.

"To the custodian, he may be the [one] . . . whose office is always filled with . . . youngsters, or who [has] . . . night meeting[s] that will necessitate keeping the building open. To older members, he may be that young fellow [who is a reminder that] . . . the church has changed so much. . . . To the nominal church member, he is the [person] . . . one can phone to learn the date Junior Day Camp begins. . . .

"To a friend, he may be the one . . . who likes golf, good music, or gardening. To the church school superintendent, [it] may be [he] . . . whose understanding strengthens his leadership and infuses it with purpose. To the chairman of the Christian education committee, he is the . . . person who shares with him the responsibility for the total educational program and is a sort of [invaluable] secretary. . . . To the pastor, the D.C.E. may be the right arm in a team ministry—one whose judgment he values, whose ability he trusts, and to whom he gives the full weight of his ministerial support. To other staff members, he may be the one who ties up the telephone ... or [shares] ... an amusing cartoon. ..." [2]

The larger urban or suburban churches employ full-time directors or ministers of religious education. In some smaller churches the director is called upon to combine his or her distinctly educational duties with other responsibilities such as those of organist, secretary, choir director, and so forth. Though this may be necessary in some churches it is often an unsatisfactory arrangement. In a very large church there may be one or more assistants who specialize in youth work, children's work, or adult work. In this case the director has the added responsibility of supervising the assistants' work.

Education and Training

Generally recommended for a DRE are four years in a liberal arts college with some courses in education-related subjects. One year or more in a graduate institution is also helpful. Many seminaries now offer courses leading to a Master in Religious Education (MRE) degree, and there are such schools as the Presbyterian School of Christian Education in Richmond, Virginia, first established to train women for educational tasks in the Presbyterian church in a day when they were not allowed to enroll in a seminary. This institution continues to be one of the major training grounds for DREs in the country—for all denominations and for both sexes. As one can see from the duties described previously, courses in psychology, sociology, recreation, and the like, as well as survey courses in the Bible and

[2] From *DCE: A Challenging Career in Christian Education* by Louise McComb. © M. E. Bratcher 1963. Used by permission of John Knox Press.

theology, are most valuable. Since there are so many DREs, there are professional organizations to which they can belong. These hold regular conferences and workshops, and give refresher courses, on-the-job training, and the opportunity to study in various fields.

Opportunities

It is impossible to know the total number of DREs now employed in local churches. The Religious Education Association estimates 40,000. The Christian Educators Fellowship (mostly Methodist) has 5,000 members. The Southern Baptist Church in 1978 reported 8,000 directors of Christian Education in their churches, with another 2,200 churches ready to hire directors. It is a growing vocation also in the Roman Catholic Church at a time when parochial schools are playing a smaller role and Sunday schools, Confraternity of Christian Doctrine (CCD) classes, and so forth are becoming more important in the education of Catholic children.

Decision on employment of education directors is made in the local church. Many denominational boards of education receive, file, and process data on qualifications and experience of applicants and will help individuals and churches get together, but they do not make selections or appointments.

For Further Information

There is a good deal of help available for a prospective education director who wishes to know what the career entails and what the opportunities are. There are two brief but excellent books. The first, *D.C.E.: A Chal-*

lenging Career in Christian Education, by Louise McComb (Atlanta: John Knox Press, 1963), is an older book, but is still a good summary of what the career is all about. A newer title is also very informative: *The D.R.E. Book,* by Maria Harris (New York: Paulist Press, 1976). This book is written from the Catholic point of view, but its overall suggestions and discussion are helpful to a person from any denomination. A prospective education director will also want to become acquainted with two organizations: The Religious Education Association, 409 Prospect, New Haven, CT 06510; and The Christian Educator's Fellowship, Box 871, Nashville, TN 37202. In addition to these organizations, guidance and direction can be obtained from the education departments or the personnel agencies of any of the denominations (see Appendix C).

DIRECTOR OF MUSIC

The formal title of a music director varies from church to church. One may be known as "choirmaster" or "choirmaster and organist" if these duties describe the position. However, if one is responsible for the overall supervision of a congregation's music program, and if the job is full time or nearly full time, one's title will likely be Director of Church Music or Minister of Music.

Responsibilities

The Minister of Music is responsible to the church for planning, conducting, and evaluating the music program of the church. He or she works with the pastor in planning the music of the congregational services, and is also responsible for the activities of the choral and instrumental groups that meet regularly. In all these activities, the skill and judgment of the Minister of Music as a musician is reflected. Knowing what to sing and how to sing it reflects his or her understanding and judgment as a musician and as a churchperson. Inseparable from the "doing" of the music is the responsibility of the Minister of Music for both planning and evaluating. Planning involves preparation—the setting of goals to be achieved, the identification and securing of needed resources (voices and instruments), the selecting of appropriate music. All of this greatly heightens the effect, the excitement, and the impact of the music when it is finally performed. Evaluation involves looking back and taking stock—measuring achievement or lack of achievement. It is a vital responsibility of the Minister of Music. Another way of describing the duties of the Director of Church Music is to list them, as many congregations do, in the following manner:

- Directs the congregation's choir(s)
- Instructs the choirs, church school classes, and sp
cial study groups in the understanding and appreciation of the liturgy, hymnody, and heritage of church
music
- Provides musical accompaniment for the congregation and choir

- Plans and directs choir schools for children
- Serves as an advisor to program committees of the congregation
- Orders the music scores for organ and choir, and supervises the maintenance of the music library
- Provides musical training for children and youth in vacation church school
- Plans and conducts services of special music during the festival seasons of the church year
- Provides music for occasional services in the parish such as weddings and funerals

Preparation and Training

Of course, adequate musical preparation is expected of a music director. For some, this begins very early in life with an interest in music and participation in music—including membership in bands, choirs, and orchestras in the home church, in high school, and in college. The experience of growing up in a church music program is invaluable to a church musician. In college it is most likely that a budding Director of Church Music will be a music major and will also take every opportunity to participate in musical organizations and thus sharpen his or her musical skills. Psychology and education courses will help these people understand the needs of the various age groups with which they will be working. One may also want to continue one's training by obtaining a master's degree in music from a college or university, or from one of the many music schools that provide specialized training.

Two other items are important in preparing to be a church musician: First, one must love music. The gift of a deep feeling for music is as important as training and education in technique. Second, one must have a concern for people. Church music is no place for a prima donna. The music director needs to have a real interest in the individual choir members (usually volunteers). To be successful in church music, one must be both flexible and patient.

Opportunities

While most churches have volunteer or part-time music help, the number of full-time positions is growing. The National Church Music Fellowship estimates twenty thousand persons are employed at least half time in churches. Admittedly, the pay scale is not what it might be, but in the music field it is almost always possible for the church musician to supplement his or her income with other activities. The hours are long but erratic. The work is frustrating at times, especially to a sensitive musician. Still, the rewards are great.

There is a growing need in the Roman Catholic Church for musicians—organists, choirmasters, and cantors. Before the Vatican Council II, the uniformity of Catholic liturgical practice made requirements and performance practices nearly the same the world over. Today every church is different, and within each parish there are varieties of liturgies and a wide number of musical forms being used. The necessity for a competent music director in each parish is growing rapidly.

For Further Information

There is a multitude of books for choir directors, organists, and church musicians available in public or school libraries, from music stores and religious bookstores. Denominational offices (see Appendix C) provide help and guidance both about the training needed for these positions and in finding the jobs available. Then there are the organizations such as the American Guild of Organists, 630 Fifth Avenue, New York, NY 10020; and the National Association of Church Musicians. Some denominations also have associations of church musicians. One such is the Presbyterian Association of Musicians (PAM), 3240 Dalrymple Drive, Baton Rouge, LA 70802. This association sponsors conferences, provides referral services, and publishes helpful materials, including a booklet, *The Work and Compensation of the Choral Musician.* PAM also publishes a brochure of guidelines for committees seeking to employ church musicians in Presbyterian churches. Other denominations have similar groups. Church musicians are hired by local churches, but much help in finding positions is available from denominations and national music organizations.

BUSINESS ADMINISTRATOR

Among the many new developments that have occurred during this generation is the increasing recognition of the need for a business administrator (CBA) as a member of the church staff. Through the years, large

12

churches have assigned administrative responsibilities to staff members. In the early fifties, the church business administrator, although his or her job title varied, began to have well-defined areas of work. The person who filled this position in the beginning often came from the business world, and performed such duties as keeping the financial records and taking care of the legal aspects of the church property. However, developments in recent years have related the work to the total program of the church, with specific assignments in the area of business administration.

The role of the church business administrator is one of service. In this role, he or she works with persons both inside and outside the church. Experience varies from limited to wide. The church business administrator works directly under the supervision of the pastor and side by side with the minister of education and the minister of music. Therefore, an ability to understand and to work with people contributes to a high degree of effectiveness.

Responsibilities

The general areas of work of the church business administrator include office management, financial administration, facilities administration, and food service operation. Because personnel are involved in each of these areas, personnel administration is also a major part of the work.

In office management, church business administrators serve as office managers for the church. They plan, direct, and coordinate all work in the church office so that all programs and the needs of leaders and members are served in the most efficient manner. The business administrator develops and maintains the organization, personnel relationships, and improved methods and procedures in business administration. The administrator is the catalyst that causes the work of the church to be carried out effectively.

In the financial administration program, the church business administrator works closely with related church officers, committees, and staff members. He or she helps to plan and install a good budget and accounting system and is responsible for its efficient operation. This person develops and recommends policies and procedures for actions related to the receiving, handling, banking, disbursing, and accounting of all church funds.

In the administration of church facilities, the church business administrator is responsible for the operational and preventive maintenance of all church properties, furniture, and equipment. He or she confers with church staff members, church officers, and committees in all matters related to building, grounds, equipment, and furniture. Insurance, legal requirements, and periodic evaluation of all properties are included in these responsibilities. The CBA plans and directs the work of all custodial and other building-maintenance personnel. He or she develops, recommends, and administers policies and procedures related to the maintenance and use of all facilities. The job also entails working with appropriate persons and groups in developing capital-budget needs and administering approved capital-budget items when purchases are made.

In the food service operation of the church, the CBA works with appropriate committees in the development of policies and procedures for efficient and economical operation. He or she supervises the kitchen personnel, and in cooperation with appropriate persons, sees that the kitchen and dining areas are properly planned, equipped, and maintained. The CBA sees that food is properly received, stored, prepared, and served with a minimum of labor and a maximum of speed. This person must assure that all food is handled in accordance with local health requirements.

The following list of duties of the church business administrator spells out the responsibilities more specifically:

• Assists the finance committee in preparing the congregation's budget
• Maintains the congregation's financial records
• Provides information and gives guidance related to the annual financial appeals
• Provides assistance that the Committee on Stewardship may need
• Assists the property committee by processing recommendations related to the acquisition and care of property and equipment
• Employs, trains, and supervises work schedules of nonprofessional church staff
• Schedules and coordinates the parish calendar
• Prepares and arranges for the printing and distribution of the congregation's news releases, business and membership correspondence, and other materials
• Serves as liaison, as directed by the pastor, in meetings of standing committees, community meetings, and public relations programs

Preparation and Training

A bachelor's degree from an accredited college with a major in business administration is recommended for this work. A person who wishes to be a church business administrator could well profit from experience in accounting, office management, business management, use of business machines, personnel management, banking, business mathematics, advertising, and law. A working knowledge of building-and-grounds maintenance and institutional food services would be helpful.

Business is the essence of the church business administrator, but it is the Lord's business and should be entered with a thorough knowledge of the various aspects of the work of the church and with a spirit of dedication to the essential purposes of the church beyond what is necessary in the ordinary business-related occupation.

Also, since the CBA works with all aspects of the church's program and the people involved in each of these, a basic understanding of people is essential. This can be gained in many ways, but courses in psychology and related subjects in college training would be helpful. Perhaps as much as in any of the local church careers, experience is a valuable teacher. Many CBAs are lured out of the business world through volunteer work in the church, which acquaints them with its satisfactions as well as with the need for good business practices within it.

Opportunities

This is one of the most steadily growing fields of local church employment. It has been estimated that there are two thousand persons now employed as full-time church business administrators. Denominational head-quarters personnel offices can help in locating new positions. Some denominations also have associations of CBAs, whose members keep each other informed of openings. There is a national organization of CBAs as well (see below).

In the Roman Catholic Church, where parish councils are becoming more important and laymen are taking responsibilities for the business affairs of the church, the position of Church Business Administrator is also beginning to take hold. (It was almost unheard of in Catholic parishes until a few years ago.)

For Further Information

As stated above, denominational offices maintain lists of jobs available in many cases, and give help in placement (see Appendix C). However, perhaps the best way to become acquainted with the opportunities is to get acquainted with a local CBA or the National Association of Church Business Administrators, P.O. Box 7181, Kansas City, MO 64113. One book about the field is entitled *Vital Church Management*, by Philip M. Larson, Jr. (Atlanta: John Knox Press, 1977).

SECRETARIAL WORK

In most local churches, the first person to be hired after the clergyman is almost always a church secretary. Some of the very smallest churches have full-time secretaries; larger churches have several, with varied duties.

17

Responsibilities

The duties of a secretary will depend upon the particular church and his or her own aptitudes. Almost any skill a secretary acquires will be useful, whether it be typing letters, planning menus, making travel reservations, arranging flowers, or bandaging a child's skinned knee. The usual duties, however, will include the following:

- Receptionist. People come to the church office for many reasons. To each of these the secretary serves as receptionist, helping everyone to have a profitable visit and feel that the church has ministered to him or her. To those people who make contact by telephone, the secretary represents the church by proficient and tactful handling of their calls.
- Stenographer-typist. Secretaries may take dictation in shorthand or transcribe from a dictaphone or handwritten notes. Theirs is the responsibility for turning the dictation into beautifully typed, technically correct letters and manuscripts, each of which will convey to the recipient the image of a church that cares.
- File clerk. The secretary is responsible for keeping all kinds of records. These include correspondence files; resource files of clippings, brochures, sermons, and promotional ideas; church membership files; business files of invoices, checks, and financial statements; and miscellaneous temporary or permanent files.
- Recorder. The secretary may be expected to record the minutes of the church council, to assist the clerk

of the church, or to serve as the clerk. He or she then types the minutes in approved style. Such minutes are the written history of the church.

• Promotional agent. Many secretaries do promotional work. This may include enlisting volunteer workers and providing materials for their training, designing special display materials, writing news stories for the local paper, directing some phase of the church program, or doing other tasks necessary for the successful completion of a planned activity.

• News editor. The church usually publishes one or more pieces of material weekly to inform, enlist, and encourage its membership. This may be printed by an outside firm or duplicated in the church office. The major responsibility for gathering and editing the materials and producing the completed product usually falls to the church secretary. Skill is needed in performing this important public relations function.

• Duplicator operator. Among items duplicated from stencils or masters cut by the secretary will be church bulletins, schedules of services, minutes of meetings, letters to the membership, curriculum materials, and special events programs. The accuracy, neatness, and attractiveness of such material is a boon to any church leader.

• Other duties. Some secretaries serve as combination secretary and bookkeeper. Some make hospital visits, plan youth fellowships, and so forth. In larger churches, two or more secretaries share the work, each doing those tasks for which they have the most aptitude. It is safe to say that whatever needs to be done in the operation of a church and its program, the secretary will have some share in it.

19

Preparation and Training

A high-school diploma is a must for any church secretary. The high-school courses should include history, English, a foreign language, human relations, and literature. These will form a broad base upon which to build special secretarial skills, which may be acquired at a business school or other specialized training institute. College is desirable, with courses in the humanities as well as in the Bible and theology to help the prospective secretary understand the church and its mission. A thorough knowledge of the church's program and the denomination to which it belongs is extremely helpful, as can be seen by studying the responsibilities we have listed.

It is truly helpful for the prospective secretary to do as much volunteer work in the church as time permits. In many cases this may be done in the office of the church, which will give one a feeling for the duties and responsibilities involved.

Before considering a position as a church secretary, or beginning training for this kind of service in the church, one might well ask the following questions, which will help one to decide whether or not to pursue this course:

• Can I accept responsibility? Church secretaries must take the responsibility for organizing their work, following through to completion on assignments, sharpening their professional skills, and entering into a caring relationship with the people of the church and community.
• Do I like people? We should be able to convey our feelings by our actions, which speak louder than

words. A church secretary should be responsive to others.

• Am I flexible? A telephone call, a visitor, or a request from a staff member can ruin a secretary's perfectly organized work schedule.

• Do I want to serve? Those who like to help people and can work behind the scenes, letting others have the limelight, have an important ingredient for the job of church secretary.

Opportunities

Good secretaries should never lack opportunities to put their skills to work. In fact, they are in constant demand. In addition to the local churches, church-related institutions and organizations employ numerous secretaries (see other chapters of this book). No one seems to have any estimate of the number of church secretaries now employed, but it comes nearer to the total number of local churches than any other position outside that of clergyman.

For Further Information

In addition to books on secretarial training, read any of the books prepared for and listed under other church occupations. Almost every one of them will be helpful in understanding the total program of the church and the various responsibilities which will at one time or another fall on the shoulders of a competent church secretary. Applications for employment are made to the local church.

PARISH WORKER

A parish worker is a local church employee; the title is used almost exclusively in the Lutheran Church, although it is known in some other denominations. This position is becoming less common as churches develop multiple staff; the duties formerly performed by the parish worker are being assumed by the Director of Religious Education, the church secretary, and the Church Business Administrator. However, there are a number of parish worker positions still occupied, and new ones are being filled each year.

Responsibilities

The parish worker is directly responsible to the pastor or clergyman and is supervised by him or her. The work entails implementing the total program of the congregation. Specific duties have sometimes been listed as follows:

- Prepares the calendar of parish activities
- Arranges for or prepares the congregation's weekly bulletin or newsletter
- Assists the pastor in the implementation of the congregation's education program
- Assists the pastor in setting up leadership courses, recruiting teachers, and coordinating the congregation's Sunday, weekday, and vacation church schools
- Assists the young people of the church to find their role in the life and mission of the congregation
- Supplements the pastor's visits to shut-ins, new-

comers to the community, the unchurched, and the members of the congregation

• May participate in community projects on behalf of the congregation as directed by the pastor and church council

Preparation and Training

In an earlier day many parish workers took special courses in Bible schools and other post-high school training institutions. The parish worker today is usually a college graduate, or at least has had some college training, including courses in religion, psychology, sociology, and education. Many of the skills required of an office secretary, education director, and church musician are valuable for a parish worker as well.

Opportunities

As indicated, the parish worker position in churches has developed into other specialities. However, the American Lutheran Church lists some two hundred parish workers now employed in this comparatively small denomination. Many times the parish worker responsibilities are combined with those of other church workers, depending on the particular skills and training of the individual.

For Further Information

See any of the information, associations, books, and materials listed for other church occupations. Lutheran Church bodies have special information available for prospective parish workers and also have an accreditation procedure for those interested. Write to the Division for Professional Leadership, Lutheran Church in America, 2900 Queen Lane, Philadelphia, PA 19129; or the Office of Support to Ministries, The American Lutheran Church, 422 South Fifth Street, Minneapolis, MN 55415.

CHRISTIAN DAY (PAROCHIAL) SCHOOL TEACHER OR PRINCIPAL

The terminology for these schools varies: Lutherans and Catholics are more likely to use the term "parochial schools," while other denominations usually call them "Christian day schools." In an earlier day, Catholic parochial schools were staffed almost entirely by priests and sisters; not so today in many dioceses. Because of the decline in the number of persons becoming members of religious orders, there is a need for many more lay teachers in Catholic schools. Also, the number of religious day schools run by other denominations has increased sharply in recent years. In many communities these may be run by a group of churches rather than one congregation, or even by an independent Christian organization set up for this purpose (see chapters 2 and 3). The largest number of schools in Protestant churches are elementary schools, although there are a few junior high and high schools as well.

Responsibilities

The work of a parochial-school classroom teacher includes first of all those responsibilities connected with any classroom situation, since these schools must meet the same standards as the state-run public schools. But coordinating education in secular subjects with religion is what the parochial-school movement is all about. Thus there are additional responsibilities for a Christian day school teacher. These have been described as follows:

• Design and develop educational experiences: stating educational objectives, selecting curriculum, developing programs, evaluating or preparing media resources
• Teach children
• Work with and teach youth: Share experiences and work with youth within the realm of their personal and church interests
• Work with families: Conduct parent-teacher conferences
• Interpret the educational program and its objectives to parents and the whole congregation

Additional functions for a principal (who is often also a teacher) would include the following:

• Coordinate the day school educational program with other programs of the congregation, and work with the educational committee.
• Administer the church day school: Manage the af-

fairs of the school; for instance, teacher recruitment and supervision.

• Work with the Education Committee by serving as advisor and resource person. This includes selecting and interpreting curriculum materials, stating educational objectives, and helping to evaluate the educational program and needs of the congregation.

• Manage finances: Develop the budget, supervise financial processes, and establish sound accounting methods.

• Manage the property: Purchase and maintain equipment, supervise maintenance, keep inventories, have insurance programs, and supervise new construction.

Training and Preparation

If one is interested in becoming a teacher or principal in a Christian day or parochial school, he should make all of the preparations necessary for a similar job in a public school—a college degree in education in one's special field of interest. In addition, a Christian school teacher needs background in religion: survey courses in the Bible and theology are necessary. There are teachers' associations in each of the denominations that have schools, and the National Association of Christian Day Schools not only provides information, but also publishes helpful materials for their teachers and conducts workshops and conventions for on-the-job training. A qualified teacher will want to spend some summer vacations in specialized religious training.

The Lutheran Church–Missouri Synod operates a college devoted almost exclusively to the training of parochial school teachers at Concordia Teachers College in River Forest, Illinois. There are many opportunities for education while teaching at such an institution and, of course, through the conferences and workshops of the teachers' associations listed below.

Opportunities

It is difficult to determine the exact number of schools and thus the job opportunities in this field for the unordained. The National Association of Christian Day Schools is in touch with some 3,865 schools who have from 2 to 50 teachers each. The Lutheran Church–Missouri Synod and the American Evangelical Lutheran Church together list 1,650 parochial schools with 8,000 teachers, while the American Lutheran Church lists over 100 schools, including kindergartens. The National Association of Christian Day Schools publishes the *Christian Teacher*, which has a teacher placement section in each issue.

For Further Information

Those interested in teaching in Roman Catholic schools should consult their own diocese for opportunities, since these schools are run on a parochial basis through the diocese. Others may gain information from the following sources:

Lutheran Education Association
Concordia Teachers College
7400 August Avenue
River Forest, IL 60305

Donald Vetter
Coordinator of Lutheran Schools
Wartburg College
Waverly, IA 50677

The American Lutheran Education Association
c/o Division of Life and Mission
American Lutheran Church
422 South 5th Street
Minneapolis, MN 55415

The National Association of Christian Day Schools
Box 550
Wheaton, IL 60187

Association of Lutheran Secondary Schools
1601 St. Joe River Drive
Fort Wayne, IN 46805

YOUTH DIRECTOR

In many larger churches there is a need for a Director or Minister of Youth. Although these positions are often filled by ordained persons, usually recent seminary graduates, in the total church career picture, such a person is more often than not unordained. In some churches the functions outlined below are carried out by the religious education director, but since the church puts a special premium on retaining the youth of its membership on its rolls, more and more congregations see the need for a separate Director or Minister of Youth.

Responsibilities

Responsibilities are as varied as the jobs to be filled, but essentially the youth director functions on the church staff as an administrator, organizer, planner, and coordinator. As she or he works with the staff and officers of the congregation to enlist adults to work with youth, the Director of Youth becomes a recruiter, discoverer, and motivator. Meeting with a youth council, the Minister of Youth functions as a director, planner, and guide. Sometimes the Youth Ministers must "do it themselves"; more often they lead others to do the job as they develop a ministry of and with youth.

In direct contact with youth, the Minister of Youth shifts into the role of enabler, counselor, encourager, and spiritual director. As problems arise, he or she acts as a catalyst for creativity, a trouble-shooter, and a referral agent.

Adult church members look to the Minister of Youth as an advisor and consultant to help them better understand and relate to young people. Youths look to the director as an example and a friend, as a mediator between the worlds of youth and adults. The youth director is also an interpreter, relating the Bible to contemporary situations.

The Minister of Youth leads young people to share the good news of the gospel with others. As people respond to the challenge of Christ, they need support, teaching, training, counsel, encouragement, friendship, and leadership. The Minister of Youth seeks to provide for these needs as he or she builds a balanced youth education program that is staffed with the finest leaders to be found.

The Director of Youth serves as a coach and guide for the young who are developing the skills and attitudes necessary for the ministry. Adults who work with youths look to the Minister of Youth for necessary leadership training.

Scheduling opportunities for wholesome recreation and fellowship with other Christians is another responsibility of the youth director. Camps, retreats, assemblies, worship, workshops, conferences, and conventions help young people reinforce their convictions and move toward Christian maturity. The Minister of Youth is often responsible for church, associational, regional, state, and convention assignments in these areas. Civic activities provide an opportunity to help create a better environment for youth in the community. Radio, television, youth music/mission tours, and other ministry projects extend the director's ministry.

Preparation and Training

Recommended academic preparation for a youth minister includes four years of training in an accredited college or university. A broad perspective should be secured with a good background in subjects such as psychology, sociology, education, philosophy, art, music, and history. Specifically religious subjects also should be studied either in college or at some other institution where one can receive specialized training. Many youth directors also have a Master of Religious Education (MRE) degree from a seminary or graduate school. Courses in recreation and physical education are useful but not essential.

To complement academic studies, it is helpful to have

worked with youth in a variety of settings during one's college days and while preparing for this work. The Minister of Youth walks with young people during the stress and storm of adolescence as they attempt to answer for themselves the big questions: Who am I? Why am I here? Where am I going? Who will go with me? What is right and wrong for me? The youth director must be close enough to these questions to appreciate them, but far enough removed to have settled them in his or her own life.

Opportunities

There are not nearly as many job openings for youth directors as for education directors in local churches. Yet the number is growing. Southern Baptists, for example, report one thousand persons in their congregations with this title, and American Lutheran congregations report over two hundred. In many other cases the work of a youth director is combined in some way with other duties on a church staff, which would suggest the wisdom of developing several abilities in preparation for this ministry.

For Further Information

Every denomination has concerns in the area of youth work, and national and regional offices can be depended on to give help to the inquirer about opportunities in this field (see Appendixes C and D). Doing religious youth work in church-related organizations can also give one both experience and help in finding opportunities for work with youth. See chapter 4 on other religious organizations for descriptions of opportunities for work with youth in such groups as YMCAs and YWCAs, Campus Crusade, Young Life, Youth for Christ, etc. Catholic work with youth is often on a diocesan rather than a parish level and information and guidance can be sought from individual dioceses or from the National Catholic Youth Organization (CYO) Federation, U.S. Catholic Conference, 1312 Massachusetts Avenue NW, Washington, DC 20005.

LIBRARIAN

In a Catholic parish where there is a parochial school, the librarian is often a staff member. This is usually a school librarian, and preparation and training as well as responsibilities are essentially the same as those for a librarian in any public school.

Congregational or parish libraries are very common and are becoming more common in both Catholic and Protestant churches. Estimates vary, but there are at least sixty thousand of these libraries in the United States. Most of them, however, are staffed by volunteers, often members of the church who are also public librarians, or by retired librarians. However, as these libraries develop, there are beginning to be openings for paid librarians on church staffs. Thus the career of church librarian is one that should be considered by anyone looking at the total picture of what is available in church work.

Responsibilities

Because this is a new breed of church career, the overall responsibilities of the church librarians have not been adequately defined by denominations. We may use as an example here a job description of such a full-time position that was listed recently by First Church of Christ Congregational in West Hartford, Connecticut, in their search for a library director for their congregation's extensive library:

The Library Director, accountable to the Library Board, plans and administers the program of library services offered by the John P. Webster Library of the First Church of Christ Congregational of West Hartford. In fulfilling these responsibilities, the director shall:

- Thoroughly investigate and study the library needs of church members and staff as well as the library needs of the greater church community in order to maximize the value of the library to these constituents
- Submit recommendations on library policies and services to the Library Board and implement policy decisions
- Consider for implementation the recommendations of library staff, such as the reference librarian or the cataloguer, as the director deems necessary for the improvement of library services
- Analyze, coordinate, and prepare budgets and control expenditures in connection with the administration of approved budgets
- Examine, select, and approve materials to be added to the library or discarded

• Approve orders for such items as books, periodicals, films, pamphlets, tapes, records, library supplies, etc., and initiate orders for capital library furniture, equipment and other items approved by the Library Board
• Interview representatives of publishers and suppliers and consult staff in the selection of needed publications, materials and equipment
• Administer personnel policies and regulations approved by the Library Board
• Interview job applicants and recommend to the Library Board employment, promotion, and termination of employment of library personnel
• Rate staff performance
• Plan and conduct staff meetings to consider library problems and to improve service
• Prepare and arrange for book reviews and lectures, teach, and hold discussions, as commonly practiced in modern libraries, and implement plans to publicize and promote library activities and services
• Assist in performing ordinary library tasks such as answering reference questions and assist in routine library duties, when needed, or in the absence of other staff members
• Attend library conferences and/or conventions for professional growth and to promote the library so that it becomes the outstanding New England church library that has been envisioned

Preparation and Training

It is recommended that a church librarian be well trained in library skills, and thus most likely would be a graduate of an accredited library school of a college or university. In addition he or she ought to have a grasp of the unique features of a church library and its ministry to the total church and community. This can be gained through association with library training programs and workshops conducted by denominations and by such organizations as the Church and Synagogue Library Association (see below). Most church librarians have first been volunteers in their congregational libraries; this is a good place to begin.

Opportunities

Full-time librarians in the local church are rare, but the opportunities are growing and this can be combined with other church occupations in a way that will make full-time employment by a congregation possible.

For Further Information

Consult the Church and Synagogue Library Association, P.O. Box 1130, Bryn Mawr, PA 19010. This is an interfaith group that publishes a regular bulletin, special guides and bibliographies, and conducts national and regional conferences and workshops for the training of church librarians. The denominations also offer special help in obtaining jobs. Two of the most active are The Lutheran Church Library Association, 122 W. Franklin Avenue, Minneapolis, MN 55405; and the Church Library Department, Southern Baptist Sunday School Board, 127 Ninth Avenue N., Nashville, TN 37234. Questions concerning libraries in the Roman Catholic Church—in both schools and parishes—should be directed to the Catholic Library Association, 461 West Lancaster Avenue, Haverford, PA 19041.

OTHER LOCAL CHURCH OCCUPATIONS

In addition to the most common church careers, which we have described, there are many other types of full-time church employment that are less common and yet offer one the possibility of having a career.

Churches that find there are special problems and thus opportunities in their communities may hire other personnel to carry out the following special ministries:

Director of Social Ministries

A Director of Social Ministries can be found on the staff of many urban churches with special needs within the community. This person is charged with the responsibility for identifying the physical and psychological needs (such as food, housing, and medical care) of the people in the congregation and community. It is the director's responsibility to develop resources and support systems between government, community, and voluntary associations to meet these needs. Such a person is usually a trained social worker as well as being grounded in religious education.

Director of Church Recreation

In larger churches the Director of Church Recreation works with the rest of the staff to provide a program of balanced recreation for parishioners of all ages. This is often most needed in the youth program of the church, but is also becoming more important as well for the senior citizens in the congregation and community. The recreation director is involved in the planning and programming of the activities for a church gymnasium or activities building of a congregation, but is also responsible for all social events (parties, banquets, fellowships, picnics, receptions, anniversaries, and the like); sports (team and tournament play), intramurals; camps, retreats, and outdoor activities; drama; arts, crafts, and hobbies; recreational music; and trips and excursions for people of all ages and divisions of the church.

Director of Children's Work

The Director of Children's Work cooperates with the other staff in a large church and is responsible for coordinating the enlisting, training, and maintaining of leadership for every organization or activity designed for children in a church. Day-care and/or kindergarten programs are often under his or her leadership. In the community, the work of this person is closely coordinated with that of the Director of Social (or urban) Ministries previously described.

Beyond these, of course, are all the support ministries of a congregation: the food service director, the engineering and custodial staff, the producers of church bulletins and other printed materials, and so forth. The complete listings of employees in the samples that follow indicate the vast variety of church careers available in the local congregation. For information on these opportunities one should apply directly to the local church.

LOCAL CHURCH PERSONNEL CHARTS

The following are the personnel descriptions for two local churches. They demonstrate the great variety of occupations possible at this level. These are not typical churches, of course, since both of them are large, complicated organizations, but they do show the many different skills needed for church work.

Riverside Church, New York, New York

Riverside Church is described because it has very large facilities ministering to the city of New York and surrounding environs, so a large support staff is needed.

• The administrative officer—business manager—of a church, along with the executive secretary, directs about a hundred employees in the following functions and occupations: There is an assistant administrative officer who supervises (a) the communications director and assistant; (b) the accounting and bookkeeping department, with six employees; (c) production support services, which include an offset printing operator, addressograph operator, and messenger/typist; and (d) receptionist activities: desk clerks, telephone operators, and central records secretary.
• The coordinator for building use and services directs the following areas: (a) housekeeping, food service, and

building upkeep (seventeen employees); (b) building maintenance and engineering functions (this group includes a chief engineer and assistant, twenty-six building engineer specialists, three parking attendants, and supervisory personnel); and (c) security, including a chief, an assistant, eight security personnel, and eleven youngsters who work part time.

• The Church School of Riverside Church, under the direction of the clergy staff, employs four department directors: preschool, children, youth, and an adult class coordinator.

• Other careers for the unordained available on the staff of Riverside Church are the following:

Director of Social Services
Director of Weekday Nursery-Kindergarten
Artistic Director of Theatre
Organist and Director of Music
Director of English Conversation
Carillonneur
Assistant Organist and Handbell Choir Director
Director of Arts and Crafts

• Riverside Church also employs a large staff of support personnel, including secretaries to the pastors and education directors, as well as other office personnel.

This comes to a grand total of 102 persons.

Central Lutheran Church, Minneapolis, Minnesota

One of the largest Lutheran churches in the United States, Central Church in its city-wide ministry employs forty-two persons. The following list of staff, supplied by the church, describes both the varied duties and the qualifications needed for these positions. The list will be of help to anyone looking for similar positions in the local church. With the exception of the senior pastor, any of the positions on this list could be held by unordained persons.

• Senior Pastor. The senior pastor's primary responsibility is to be the spiritual head of the congregation, to act as the executive director for the overall administration of all phases of congregational worship and of all church programs, to provide various forms of worship, education, and evangelism for the spiritual life and growth of the congregation.

• Life and Growth Pastor. This pastor's primary responsibility is to provide for the spiritual life and growth of the congregation through the effective integration of new members into the congregation and the development of ministries and programs designed to meet the needs of the congregation for fellowship, servanthood, and specialized education.

• Parish Education Pastor. The main responsibility of the Parish Education Pastor is to provide leadership and direction for the educational ministry of this congregation. This involves being responsible for the Sunday School program, teaching in the confirmation ministry, involvement with and supervision of the youth ministry, and responsibility for programming adult education courses, and teaching classes as determined by the pastoral staff.

• Program Pastor. The basic responsibility of this post is to provide leadership and direction in the areas of outreach evangelism, young adult ministry, worship, and programs for Sunday Evening at the Central Church.

• Urban Ministry Pastor. The primary responsibility of the Urban Ministry Pastor is to enable the realization of the reconciling and redeeming character of the gospel in the context of the urban situation. Among other functions, this involves responsibility for exercising care for those not now being reached by the church, serving as liaison between the church and those groups alienated from traditional metropolitan society, and awakening concern on occasions of crisis.

• Business Administrator. The Business Administrator must manage the business activities of the church and the properties belonging to the church and supervise the support staff. QUALIFICATIONS: college degree with a major in business administration or its equivalent preferred; capabilities of leadership, communications, and tactfulness essential; experience in church business administration preferred; concern for and sensitivity to people and the church also needed.

• Secretary/Receptionist. The secretary to the business administrator is in charge of the information desk and answers the telephone. QUALIFICATIONS: knowledge of general office procedures; abilities in typing and use of office equipment; high-school diploma with some advanced training; skills in writing, grammar, and sentence structure; clear and pleasant voice for telephone work; concern for and sensitivity to people and the church; pleasing personality and an ability to work with others.

• Communications Director. This position involves being responsible for printed communications. QUALIFICATIONS: college degree with a major in journalism or its equivalent; experience in preparing copy, writing, and editing; expertise in sentence structure, spelling, and punctuation; artistic sense for layout; concern with and sensitivity to people and the church; pleasing personality and the ability to work with others.

• Printer (part-time). The printer operates and maintains the print shop. QUALIFICATIONS: high school diploma, graduate of a vocational/technical institute with a major in printing, or equivalent experience; experience in design, layout, and graphics; experience in a commercial print shop desirable.

• Building Supervisor. This post entails responsibility for the care and maintenance of the buildings, equipment, and grounds. QUALIFICATIONS: second-class driver's license; experience in several of the following areas: supervision of others; ability to perform a variety of repairs; knowledge of plumbing, electric wiring, heating, cooling, and ventilating systems; understanding of blueprints and specifications; ability to use cleaning equipment, including floor-cleaning equipment; and knowledge of maintenance practices.

• Custodian. The custodian assists the building supervisor.

• Night Custodian. The night custodian also assists the building supervisor.

• Housekeeper. This job also involves helping the building supervisor.

• Financial Secretaries. These secretaries are responsible for the financial records of the congregation.

• Food Service Director. This director is responsible for the general food service. QUALIFICATIONS: formal training and/or experience in institutional food preparation; pleasing personality, and an ability to work with others.

• Music Director. The primary responsibility of the Music Director is to provide and coordinate supportive music for the programs of Central Lutheran Church. QUALIFICATIONS: a commitment to the church, the body of Christ, and a desire to participate in Christian community as a means of demonstrating and communicating the Christian faith; training and experience in Christian church music; a familiarity with Christian worship, especially as it is expressed in the Lutheran liturgies and other forms of worship; a sensitivity to and an understanding of the basic dynamics of interpersonal relationships, and the ability to use these skills creatively and supportively in fulfilling the responsibilities of this position; an ability to plan, develop, and implement music programs.

• Music Secretary (part time).

• Librarian. The librarian is responsible for the libraries, book nook, and boutique. QUALIFICATIONS: knowledge of library science; experience in a multimedia center helpful; appreciation of books and wide range of interests; pleasing personality, and the ability to work with others; concern for and sensitivity to people and the church.

• Secretary (ies). Secretaries to the individual pastor (s). QUALIFICATIONS: See Secretary/Receptionist.

• Parish Education Director. The primary responsibility of the Parish Education Director is for the Christian education of children through grade seven. QUALIFICATIONS: a demonstrated commitment to Christ and the ability to articulate a personal faith statement; a commitment to the church, the body of Christ, and a desire to participate in the Christian community as a means of demonstrating and communicating the Christian faith; training and experience in Christian education; a demonstrated ability or capability to teach and to share the Person of Christ, Scriptures, and the Christian faith as expressed in the Lutheran tradition.

• Volunteer Services Coordinator. This is the supervisor and coordinator of the Volunteer Services Program. QUALIFICATIONS: High school diploma, with some advanced training; knowledge of personnel techniques; abilities in general administration and supervision; skills in group process and orientation; concern for and sensitivity to people and the church; pleasing personality, and the ability to work with others.

• Youth Director. The primary responsibility of the Youth Director is to supervise the Youth Ministry of Central Lutheran Church. This person seeks to involve youth, grade seven and beyond, and adults in a cooperative ministry that proclaims Jesus as Lord, and recognizes that growth in grace and commitment to Christ is a lifelong process. Growth in grace is of special importance during the formative years of young adulthood. QUALIFICATIONS: a sensitivity to the needs, desires, joys, hurts, etc. of people, especially youth, and a willingness to affirm the personhood of each individual; must be one who enjoys being with and working with youth; an ability to plan, develop and implement programs for young adults. (See also Parish Education Director.)

2

Careers in Church-Wide Institutions and Offices

Beyond the local church perhaps the next logical sphere of career opportunities in religion is the institutions run by denominations or faith groups, and the offices and program activities of those groups.

Every church body has a national headquarters, where there are many career opportunities in a wide variety of fields. In addition most groups have regional offices under various names such as diocese, synod, presbytery, and so on, depending on the nomenclature of the church. Many times these regional offices are concerned with program activities to a greater extent than the larger national office.

There are also thousands of career opportunities in the institutions or programs under the supervision of a denomination or church body. This chapter examines these opportunities, and breaks them down into the following areas: education, health and welfare, social action, youth work, research, church extension, communication and publishing, camping and retreats, and administration. Besides these, there are many careers or vocations possible in the lay orders of the Roman Catholic, Episcopal, Lutheran, and some other church groups. Finally, one ought to examine the careers possible in specialized ministries, which are found in lay training, charismatic services, renewal activities, historical commissions, and a host of other miscellaneous programs carried out by denominations and faith groups.

EDUCATION

The church has always taken seriously the injunction of Christ—often referred to as "The Great Commission"—when he sent his followers out: "Go therefore and make disciples of all nations. . . . teaching them . . ." (Matt. 28 : 19–20). In European countries where the church was almost always a state institution, religion was a part of every classroom curriculum. When these churches were transplanted to the New World, among the first establishments were schools or colleges for the training of clergy and church workers. In every congregation or parish the Sunday school or parochial school is established as soon as there is a congregation. Every denomination lists schools on every level. Teaching within these schools and the supervision of their personnel, as well as the preparation of materials for use in these schools, is one of the largest areas of work sponsored by a church body. Thus there are also thousands of opportunities for careers in these educational pursuits.

Teachers

In chapter 1, Careers in the Local Church, we also touch on the need for teachers in the parochial or Christian day schools on that level. Many of these schools, particularly the high schools, are run by a group of churches of one, or sometimes more than one, denomination. Training and education for these posts would be the same as that for teachers in the public school on the same level, with additional need for a background in religion. Further information on opportunities for teaching in such schools can be obtained by writing the associations suggested in the section, Christian Day (Parochial) School Teachers or Principals, chapter 1.

There are also many opportunities for teaching careers sponsored by church groups in colleges and universities. Most of the first colleges in the United States were established by religious bodies to train the clergy, as we have noted. Even later, when these schools' purpose broadened, religious bodies continued to found many colleges, usually liberal arts institutions.

Many of these church-originated colleges have long since become altogether independent, maintaining no ties with any religious bodies. Even these, however, often maintain a religion department. Some other colleges have maintained their church-related status, and the denominations are active in their support of these institutions. The person looking for a career in teaching who feels a commitment to Christianity certainly would do well to investigate the many possibilities for teaching in one of these institutions. Even in the most strictly denomination-oriented schools, however, the pluralism of America is making itself known in the student bodies of these institutions, and the general approach in all classes, although religion-oriented, is much broader.

Preparation for teaching on the college level will depend entirely on the specific subject or disciplines to be taught. An advanced degree—usually a Ph.D.—is almost a necessity in all fields, even those that deal specifically with theology and religious studies.

Information about the whole area of careers in teaching in religious-oriented colleges can be obtained from the Council of Protestant Colleges and Universities, 1818 R Street NW, Washington, DC 20036; the Commission on Higher Education of the National Council of Churches, 475 Riverside Drive, New York, NY 10027; or the board of education of the denomination concerned (see Appendix C). Information about Roman Catholic colleges can be obtained from the Department of Higher Education of the U.S. Catholic Conference, 1312 Massachusetts Avenue NW, Washington, DC 20005; or the National Catholic Education Association, Dupont Circle NW, Washington, DC 20036. Another source of information about teaching religion in colleges is the American Academy of Religion, Dr. John Priest, Executive Director, Florida State University, Tallahassee, FL 32306.

Mission School Teachers

Mission schools under the supervision of national boards of home missions have been organized and maintained in many special situations. In general these schools are found in areas where minority groups—blacks, Hispanics, American Indians—live, or where there are young people in families who live in isolated areas and whose income is low, or in families of migrant workers in various parts of the country. The boards of home missions endeavor to furnish these young people with a good education in a setting that seeks Christian commitment from them. These schools thus offer career opportunities to qualified teachers who wish not only to teach, but to express their Christian faith through their teaching. Information about opportunities can be secured from the offices of missionary personnel in national denominations listed at the end of this chapter or the National Council of Churches or National Association of Evangelicals (see chapter 3).

Teachers in Homes

There are also opportunities for teaching children in homes for children under the direction of home mission or social welfare boards. (See the section on Social Welfare in this chapter.) If they are Roman Catholic, these institutions are often under the sponsorship and supervision of, or related to, a religious order within that church. (See the section of this chapter on religious orders.) Many of these institutions are for the unfortunate, handicapped, or neglected children who need institutional care, at least for a time. These homes offer education and loving, mature care so that the individuals in the institution will be able to develop as far as possible as if they were in a caring and responsible family. Teachers are needed who have a special interest in and capability for dealing with children. Teachers must also have specialized training to help these children help themselves. Further information can be had from the administrators of the child-care institutions involved or the social welfare board of the sponsoring denomination or order.

Prep Schools

In the area of teaching, one should not overlook the possibility of teaching in prep schools—sponsored mostly by the Roman Catholic or Episcopal churches, at least in this country. A few such schools are run by other denominations or on an interchurch basis. All are tightly controlled, close-knit institutions—usually boarding schools—that include daily chapel services and often military training as part of the curriculum. Usually the faculty of the school comes from the sponsoring church group. Information can be obtained by writing to the individual schools, the Catholic or Episcopal dioceses concerned, or the national offices: Department of Elementary and Secondary Education, U.S. Catholic Conference, 1312 Massachusetts Avenue NW, Washington, DC 20005; National Association of Episcopal Schools, 815 Second Avenue, New York, NY 10017. Information on prep schools is also available from the Council for Religion in Independent Schools, 107 South Broad Street, Kennett Square, PA 19348. This is an association of 719 headmasters plus 700 chaplains in prep schools under Catholic, Protestant, and Jewish sponsorship.

Campus Ministries

In recent years the church has looked to its responsibility for the university and college communities and has sought to redefine its ministry there. On the campus the church is represented by chaplains involved in counseling, worship, recreation, and education. Many of these campus workers are ordained clergy. However, many are not, and thus there are many opportunities here for personnel who have the qualifications to work with college students as the latter are educated and trained, and in the process "find themselves" in relation to their inner life and faith.

Campus ministries usually bear denominational labels, although often there is a great deal of cooperation between the representatives of different faiths on the campus, particularly in stateowned institutions, where this ministry cannot be officially sponsored by the college or university. Persons preparing themselves for this kind of work ought to have a strong background in religion, but must also be flexible enough to deal with the multitude of approaches to life that one finds on the average campus today. The type of training that is required for counselors or teachers in other non-religious fields is appropriate for campus religious workers as well.

Information about these ministries and job openings can be obtained from the higher education office of any of the denominations listed at the end of this chapter; from the National Council of Churches; National Association of Evangelicals; from the Catholic Campus Ministry Association, 780 Student Center building, Wayne State University, Detroit, MI 48202; or from an interfaith organization, The National Institute for Campus Ministries, 885 Centre Street, Newton, MA 92159.

Other careers offered through denominational channels and related to education such as departmental executives, field representatives, developers, and writers of curriculum are treated in other sections of this chapter.

HEALTH AND WELFARE

Taking its cue from the ministry of Jesus, the church has continued to be interested in healing ministries in a wide variety of circumstances and backgrounds. Since the church ministers to people, their physical and mental well-being is one of its major concerns. Institutions and programs to deal with the sick and the needy were among the first priorities of the church in the United States. Usually the scope of these institutions and programs extends beyond the capability of a local church, and it falls rather to groups of churches or denominations and church bodies to fill this need—which they have done and continue to do.

Many of the oldest and best hospitals and related institutions in this country (see below) were established by religious groups, denominations, or orders. Most of them continue to be rather closely tied with their sponsors, since the principle of ministering to the whole person, or "holistic" medicine, has become more prominent. Persons with a religious commitment will look to these institutions for possible career opportunities.

There are many different types of such institutions, and they offer an infinite variety of career possibilities. Some of the most obvious will be treated here, but closer investigation will uncover a multitude of other occupations that are available in these institutions. (See also chapter 3, Careers in Interdenominational and Interfaith Councils and Agencies, as well as chapter 4, Careers in Non Church-Related Organizations.)

Many of the jobs offered by church-sponsored institutions and programs overlap in their descriptions and qualifications. And they are found in a wide variety of institutions such as hospitals; nursing homes; homes for senior citizens; children's homes; homes for the mentally retarded or mentally ill; homes and programs for the blind, the deaf, and other physically handicapped persons; special urban ministries, ministries to migrant workers; halfway houses; and dozens of institutions that defy classification or call for very specialized ministries for unusual situations. In all of these there is need for personnel who fulfill a number of different requirements. Most of the positions can be filled by unordained but trained people.

Hospital Personnel

The most obvious need in all these institutions is for doctors. Of the approximately 250,000 physicians in the U.S., most are in private practice either as general practitioners or as specialists. Out of some 34,000 physicians who are residents or interns in hospitals, about 24,000 are employed in church-related hospitals. Also, of the some 10,000 others who hold regular positions on hospital staffs, many also do some work in church-related institutions. Information about becoming a physician is of course obtainable from the usual medical sources, but the person considering service in a religious institution will want to investigate its sponsorship and religious orientation as well.

Nurses are needed in abundance in religious hospitals and other healing institutions. In fact, many of these institutions have been a major source of trained nurses in the past. As the degree program for nurses becomes more and more widespread and more often required, however, these institutions have affiliated themselves with colleges and universities in cooperative programs. Nursing is applicable in many of the institutions of the church and other religious groups.

Nurses who desire to work under Christian auspices both on this continent and overseas will often find themselves in relatively isolated sections of the country or in institutions that minister to a wide variety of needs. This means that the resident nurse may be required to do many jobs other than traditional bedside nursing—such as midwifery, dental education, and even practicing general medicine.

Most of the larger denominations have information available on the need for nurses in their institutions and tell something about where to go for training and how to gain experience (see Appendixes C, D, and E).

Besides doctors and nurses, there is a need in all medical institutions for a large number of other personnel: medically trained staff such as radiologist, anesthesiologist, cardiologist, pharmacist, physical therapist, and many more, as well as such related support staff occupations of manager, buyer, accountant, secretary, and maintenance person.

Information on church-related hospitals and homes can be obtained from each denomination's headquarters listed at the end of this chapter, or from such groups as the American Protestant Hospital Association, 840 North Lake Shore Drive, Chicago, IL 60611; or the Catholic Hospital Association, 1428 South Grand Boulevard, St. Louis, MO 63014.

Social Welfare Institutions

Like those in hospitals, ministries of social welfare are very diverse. Religious people founded and continue to staff these institutions, and the committed person looking for a career of true service to humanity ought to investigate these possibilities carefully. The personnel needs at these institutions are varied because the types of people they serve are, too.

Most denominations have some kind of ministry for those less fortunate than most of us. Traditionally this has meant schools and homes for the blind, the deaf, and other persons with sensory impairments, as well as mentally retarded or disturbed people. Since there still exists a need for personnel in such institutions, there are careers to be pursued along these lines. Those interested in serving in this way should have training in the specialized field in which they will be working. However, more recently the trend in ministries of this kind has been to work toward helping the handicapped take their place in society as much as possible. Thus the homes for the blind and deaf, for example, are fewer than in the past, but the special work involved in training these persons to find useful employment and create a satisfactory life is still very much a part of the church's ministry. People interested in finding out more about this kind of employment should consult the directory of their own denomination (see Appendix C) or write for information to such groups as The Ephphatha Services, a church-affiliated services-program agency for the sensory-impaired run by the American Lutheran Church, P.O. Box 713, Sioux Falls, SD 57101; or the National Apostolate for the Mentally Retarded (Catholic), P.O. Box 4588, Trinity College, Washington, DC 20017.

Social Workers

Social workers are being employed in increasing numbers by many church-related agencies in an attempt to broaden their ministries to include the community in which they are located. In the inner city, where the needs of the community are diverse and multidimensional; in subcultures, such as those involving drug sale and abuse; in the suburban areas, where alienation is high and families are in crisis; in all of these and in many more places, the skills of social workers are being utilized.

The requirements for social work include a college or university degree in the social sciences, followed by additional course work or a master's degree in social work (MSW). In many cases, of course, the social worker will specialize in certain areas of study to enhance his or her skill. Information about opportunities in this field is available from any denomination or church office (see Appendix C). In many cases, because there is a special need to encourage people to enter social work ministries, there are also training scholarships available (write denominational offices).

Counseling Centers

Another recent extension of the Christian ministry has involved the development of church-sponsored counseling centers. In rare instances these centers are attached to a local church, such as the one at the Marble Collegiate Church in New York City, which is integrally related to the pastoral ministry of that congregation. Most, however, are denominationally sponsored. In many cases the staffs of these centers are pastoral counselors and thus usually clergy, but a number of trained, unordained counselors are needed, and persons interested in a counseling career should investigate the opportunities in this field.

In a large counseling center there are apt to be one or more psychiatrists on the staff who work at least part-time. But most of the persons who serve as counselors have received other counseling training and experience from a variety of institutions and organizations. In many cases the counseling center is attached to denominational social service agencies that deal with a variety of related problems and conditions such as the adoption of children, alcohol treatment, and so on. All of these centers, however, are in need of religion-oriented counseling personnel.

Clinical counseling training is now a part of most seminary courses, and is also offered by other institutions to those not seeking ordination. For further information consult the social welfare board or department of any denomination listed at the close of this chapter or for general advice and information write to the Council for Clinical Training or the Department of Ministry of the National Council of Churches. Both are located at 475 Riverside Drive, New York, NY 10027.

Halfway Houses

Halfway houses include a number of ministries that seek to be available to persons halfway between certain institutions and the community; that is, those leaving an institution such as a mental hospital and reentering the community. Probably the origins of this approach are in sheltered workshops and centers for crippled or retarded workers. Now a rather broad spectrum of such agencies is developing to cope with problems of alcoholism, drug addiction, and delinquency, or to help persons returning to society after serving a prison sentence. Many such institutions are run on a community or interchurch basis, but some also are run by one church body, especially those affiliated with the Roman Catholic Church.

Not quite in the same category, but certainly related to the halfway-house approach, are the gang workers and others who seek to work with "dropout" youths in their mobile and highly explosive society. Some workers in large cities move out into the streets and attach themselves to a group. Others move into the areas where there are clearly defined congregations of youths who are neither working nor in school, and seek to establish outposts of communication. Many times these workers use a refurbished house that a group of concerned and interested citizens under the sponsorship of a group of church denominations has taken over in a run-down district.

Ministries to the Down-and-Out

On an established level, the Salvation Army (properly called a denomination, since it has congregations and is organized as a church) is best known for its work with the dispossessed, the alcoholic, the addicted, the poor, and the unfortunate. The work of the "Army" is changing, too, but the citadels and outposts it staffs are still there and are looking for personnel. The greatest number of full-time employees of the Army are enlisted as officers, but there is also a large need for corps program assistants in the eleven hundred corps-community centers in the United States that provide a wide range of services to millions of people of diverse age, race, economic status, and culture. Information on employment can be obtained by writing to the Candidates Secretary, The Salvation Army, at any of these addresses: 120 West 14th Street, New York, NY 10011; 1424 Northeast Expressway, Atlanta, GA 30329; 860 North Dearborn Street, Chicago, IL 60610; or 30840 Hawthorne Boulevard, Rancho Palo Verdes, CA 90274.

Information about similar missions to the needy is available from other denominations at their headquarters or regional offices. Several religious orders for both men and women in the Roman Catholic Church specialize in this type of ministry and should be investigated by anyone interested in devoting a lifetime to it (see also the section, Religious Orders, in this chapter).

Working with Older People

Geriatrics is an area in which churches have been interested for many years. It is also expanding, and the whole concept of what is needed is changing. For a long time there have been "sunset" homes, or homes for the aged with accompanying nursing homes, to care for those who are unable to care for themselves. There are still thousands of such homes run by churches—usually by a group of churches of one denomination—and they remain in need of staff of all types.

However, the need for geriatric workers has multiplied as the average age of the population has increased and many people have retired under Social Security. The whole approach to the treatment of the elderly has been scrutinized by the church and religious institutions. The newer homes for the aged have been planned to make it possible for older people to take care of themselves as much as possible. Recreation and educational programs have been established not just to keep hands busy, but to give meaning to life. Thus there has come into being the need for more and better-trained staff at these institutions.

New opportunities are opening all the time to work with older people, particularly in areas with a large retirement population and more "leisure villages," as they are often euphemistically called, are developing. Often a local church is not able to cope with a ministry of this kind; thus denominations are beginning to take notice of the need and are hiring staff to counsel and work with older people in many areas of the country. Some denominations have established special commissions to deal with the subject of geriatrics: Part of their function is to train personnel.

Workers among Minorities

The areas of the country where minorities are living and need special help in making adjustments to their environment are usually also the places where the church does not have congregations and parishes—or those that are there do not have the financial backing to support special ministries to these people. Thus there have developed ministries to minorities. Departments of urban research exist denominationally and cooperatively to strengthen the work of ministries within cities. Sometimes people skilled in urban ecology are employed as consultants; at other times such people are made a part of a permanent staff. Information can be obtained on the possibilities for careers in urban work from the departments of urban ministries listed by most denominations. Or one can obtain information from the urban training centers that have been established in several cities.

SOCIAL ACTION

To a greater or lesser degree the church has always been engaged in social change. To many people this is only peripheral to the church's mission. They believe that the message of the church changes individuals, who in turn, in their own way, work for change in their environment. Yet to some extent every church body is actively involved in a social action program, working with government organizations and other institutions to bring about equality of opportunity, relief from poverty, and other positive changes.

Nearly every denomination has a department or commission of this type that is working toward social change for the good of all humankind. These departments are usually quite small, even within the largest and most socially active denominations. There are few careers available in this area; nevertheless it ought to be explored by one whose interests lie along this line. A number of training centers in the U.S. have formed the Action Training Coalition to provide instruction in urban issues for church professionals. Some of these centers, Center for Urban Training (CUT) in Toronto, Metropolitan Urban Services Training (MUST) in New York City, and Metropolitan Association of Philadelphia (MAP), have interesting acronyms as titles, but all are similar in their purpose: to help church professionals become aware of the dynamics of society by enhancing their understanding of it. The prime purpose of these centers is to train people to work in their own vocation. A few persons also will want to make training a ministry.

Among the denominations there are some that have been especially active in this area. Persons within those denominations or those wanting to work in this field should consult the following places for more information about what is being done and what can be done to develop new careers in social action:

Baptist Joint Committee on Public Affairs
200 Maryland Avenue NE
Washington, DC 20002

Justice and Peace Center (Catholic)
3900 North Third Street
Milwaukee, WI 53212

Lutheran Human Relations Association
Valparaiso University
Valparaiso, IN 46383

National Center for Urban Affairs
1521 16th Street NW
Washington, DC 20036

Unitarian-Universalist Service Committee
78 Beacon Street
Boston, MA 02108

United Methodist Church Board of Church and
Society
100 Maryland Avenue NE
Washington, DC 20002

United Church of Christ
Center for Social Action
297 Park Avenue South
New York, NY 10010

In addition, one can obtain information on a number
of social action programs from these denominational
peace fellowships (see, too, Appendix E for more
information):

Catholic Peace Fellowship
Box 271
Nyack, NY 10960

Disciples Peace Fellowship
Box 1986
Indianapolis, IN 46206

Episcopal Peace Fellowship
61 Gramercy Park North
New York, NY 10010

WORK WITH YOUTH

Work with youth is often closely related to work in
health and welfare. Since this is a larger task involving a

greater investment of time and money than most individual churches can handle, youth work is often done under the sponsorship of a group of churches, usually a regional division of one denomination.

One of the most active in this field is the Roman Catholic Church, in which youth work is usually under diocesan sponsorship. The U.S. Catholic Conference maintains a division for youth work: The National Catholic Youth Organization Federation (NCYOF). It provides ministry services and an opportunity for Catholic youth leadership to work with affiliated dioceses throughout the country. The NCYOF program emphasizes an approach to parish youth that is spiritual, cultural, recreational, social, and community-service oriented. There are numerous career opportunities here for both national and youth office staff, who are concerned with retreats, athletics, counseling, and leadership training, as well as with encouraging local parishes to hire and train youth ministers. For most jobs a college degree and some youth ministry experience on a local level are required. In addition, training in theology, group dynamics, program development, and management of people is desirable. In a recent survey, CYO reported three hundred youth workers on their national staff, and five hundred under diocesan sponsorship.

Youth ministries are a growing phenomenon in other churches as well. Most denominations have an office of youth ministries that helps congregations see the potential for youth work in the areas where they live. In addition, these youth officers are involved with related activities such as the denomination's camping and retreat programs. Youth officers also help to plan regional and national gatherings of youth for inspiration and training. More information can be obtained from the youth offices of denominations listed at the end of this chapter.

RESEARCH

Research workers are employed full time in increasing numbers by church-related colleges, theological seminaries, denominational boards, and by local, state, and regional divisions of the church. (See also chapter 3, Interdenominational and Interfaith Councils and Agencies.)

Research work is often related to the establishment of new congregations and cooperative planning with other denominations, but the facilities of a research office are used by every division of a national church body. Work at this office may include many projects in religious education, psychology, home and foreign missions, international relief, refugee problems, statistics, communication, administration, and organization.

A person interested in doing research needs certain personal qualifications. He or she needs a high degree of perspective on the institutions of religion. One is required to appraise and evaluate objectively the numerical information or data gathered, and must look at the decline and fall as well as the rise and growth of religious programs and institutions. One must be able to recognize, through the facts presented, what churches cannot do as well as what they can do.

Training and preparation for these positions usually require both a college degree and an advanced degree or training in the subjects to be researched. Some help in determining the extent of a denomination's need and the possibilities for employment in this field can be provided by denominational offices (see Appendix C). Since research is a comparatively new field, however, and information may be hard to come by, one ought to investigate also what can be gleaned from the *Journal of the Religious Research Association,* Box 228, Cathedral Station, New York, NY 10025. Some information may also be available from state and local councils of churches and from the Department of Research and Survey, National Council of Churches, 475 Riverside Drive, New York, NY 10027.

CHURCH EXTENSION AND EVANGELISM

Although the peak of the building and establishing of new churches was reached in the late forties and early fifties, much of the planning and work of denominations continues to be involved in winning new converts and spreading the work of the church into new communities, those it has not yet reached. Much of this is done by ordained personnel, of course, and the work (in a new community) revolves around the clergyman who conducts the program. However, there is a need for unordained personnel of various kinds in the planning and building stages of new churches and in the direction of the work from the central or district headquarters of a church body.

Usually a survey of the new community is necessary, and cooperative planning with other denominations is called for. In the early stages of the development of a congregation, the denomination may provide the salary of an education director, a church secretary, or a parish worker, who can do much of the detailed work of the business of the church and leave the clergyman free for calling and pastoral work.

The approaches to both church extension and evangelism are changing. The church now looks more thoroughly at a community and tries to assess its total needs. Thus, the program that is established is more varied than in the past, and more diverse kinds of people are needed on the staff.

Each denomination has a different approach to the work of church extension and evangelism, but there are careers for the unordained that should be investigated. Write to the Board of Home Mission, National Mission, or Homeland Mission (the terminology varies) of the denomination involved. See the list at the end of this chapter.

CAMPS AND RETREATS

One of the largest sources of both part- and full-time career opportunities in religion is in the hundreds of camps and retreats run by the church and other religious organizations. The American Camping Association says there are some three thousand camps and retreats in the United States run under religious auspices. Many of these are managed by non-church-related groups; these are discussed in chapter 4. However, a great many of them are denominationally owned and operated. Usually the actual ownership is in the hands of a corporation, with a board of managers from the region, but most denominations act in a supervisory capacity to all of the camps or retreat centers owned by congregations or regional associations. Information concerning these is usually available from the denomination's headquarters (see Appendix C).

Camps

One of the most active denominations supporting camping activity is the American Lutheran Church. Their program will be used here as an example of the type conducted by most denominations. There are sixty-five camp corporations related to this church body. They vary widely in their organization, yet their supervision is headed by the Director of National Ministries from the division of life and mission of the American Lutheran Church, 422 South Fifth Street, Minneapolis, MN 55415.

The full-time staff usually includes a camp director. In addition, there is often a resident camp manager, a number of part- or full-time counselors, and other support staff during the busy seasons, including cooks, grounds keepers, and carpenters. At one church-related camp, the work of a camp director has been outlined as follows: The camp director is an administrator, an educator with an informal approach, and a community organizer. Specifically, the duties are spelled out:

The camp director shall:

• Develop basic business procedures for carrying out correspondence, bookkeeping, record keeping, and filing
• Develop budgets, capital and operational
• Develop proper procedures for use and maintenance of property
• Purchase equipment, food, and supplies

- Have the insurance program reviewed annually by an objective broker
- Develop a comprehensive plan for land development which allows the best land use and balance and allows each building maximum flexibility
- Recruit, train, and supervise staff

In a larger camp some of these duties are carried out by assistants who may be resident camp managers, full-time program directors, and the like, or by part-timers from the staffs of the groups using the camp.

Training for the position of camp director has been suggested as follows: Get work experience during college in one or more camps. Let the camp director know that you are interested in camping as a career. Being a camp director is a general type of position, and requires a wide variety of capabilities. For training, look within the church, social agencies, and governmentally financed camping programs. The jobs available combine all kinds of tasks, but the person planning to make camping a career should focus on these questions:

- Can I deal responsibly with people?
- Can I handle money entrusted to me by an organization?
- Can I work well with and be sensitive to a broad spectrum of people: adults, older people, handicapped, minorities, children?
- Do I appreciate land and its use and see the possibilities of people learning on land?
- Am I enough of a self-starter to be able to initiate and carry out programs involving other people without being supervised?

Retreat Centers

In contrast to camps, which are usually seasonal or part time and which serve large groups—generally of the same age or with a common interest—retreat centers are smaller operations. Their programs are more intimate, and often educational. Most retreats are open year-round; small groups of people from individual congregations or geographical areas come for a short time to study together and learn through group experience.

Some of these retreats are under the sponsorship of non–church-related groups, but many are denominationally sponsored, and cater almost exclusively to people of one denomination. Retreats came into being early in the twentieth century and developed rather rapidly. Many were established by orders or groups within the church as special training grounds for their own members. Others were set up because some property was given to the church that included a mansion or large home that could easily be converted into a center to house groups. Most of these retreat centers do not have programs of their own, but provide the facilities for religious groups to bring in their leadership and set up a program for the duration of their stay. On the other hand, there are some larger retreat centers (such as those discussed in chapter 4) that do have full-time program staff.

There are career opportunities for a retreat manager, sometimes for a teacher or program director, and sufficient support staff in the way of secretaries, registrars, accountants, housekeepers, cooks, and maintenance personnel.

One of the most active denominations in providing this kind of facility for church groups is the Episcopal

Church, which lists over one hundred such retreats and conference centers under its sponsorship. Almost every denomination has centers of this kind, with career opportunities available to those interested in this kind of career. See Appendix E.

COMMUNICATIONS

One of the largest programs of any denomination is in the field of communication: publishing, public relations, radio, TV, and related activities. In this area the need is great for writers, editors, reporters, broadcasters, and public relations and advertising people—all of whom are engaged in exciting and rewarding careers directly related to their Christian commitment. In most denominations, these activities are under the aegis of the publication division, which may include an official publishing house. Often the public relations activities are more directly related to the executive departments of the church. Jobs requiring contact with radio and television may be found in both areas. Many of the careers described below cross over into several areas of the communication program conducted by the churches. (See also the descriptions of similar kinds of work in chapter 3, Careers in Interdenominational and Interfaith Councils and Agencies, as well as those in chapter 4, Careers in Non–Church-Related Organizations.)

Publishing

Printing and Related Work. Printing is involved in a number of denominational operations. A list of official church publishing houses is found at the end of this section. Many of these do not maintain their own printing plants, but those that do need all of the skills involved in the process: typesetting, platemaking, and press works, plus the accompanying art and design. Training in these skills is offered in high schools, vocational schools, and technical institutes. The usual way to enter the skilled printing vocation, however, is by serving an apprenticeship in print shops over a period of years. Persons with an aptitude for this type of work should investigate the possibilities in a church-owned publishing house with its own printing facilities. In addition to the composing room, press room, and binding operation, these plants need such support personnel as secretaries, bookkeepers, and accountants, as well as managers of each of these operations.

Whether publishing companies have their own printing plants or not, publishing is one of the main activities of religious bodies, especially of the larger ones. Denominational houses publish literature for use in religious education, including Sunday schools, weekday schools, parochial schools, and informal classes. These publishers produce and sell religious books of general interest for all age groups, as well as a host of other related materials such as visual aids, ecclesiastical arts materials, church furniture, and the like. For this, many different types of skills are needed.

Writers. In every publishing house there are some people involved primarily in writing. Writers are needed for church-sponsored magazines; to put together curriculum materials; to write books (although sometimes this is done by free-lancers not on the staff), advertising copy, and other promotional materials; and

72

so on. The religious journalist is an important and essential cog in the wheel of publishing. Those interested
in a career in writing should take college journalism
courses, and have a background in religion and some
experience in writing, which can be gained in a number
of ways, such as working on a college newspaper or
yearbook, or writing for a paper in a small town.

Editors. All religious publishing houses have editors
and assistant editors on their staff. These people also
work for religious journals and magazines. N. W. Ayer
and Son's annual directory lists one thousand four hundred religious periodicals in the United States. A good
many need at least one editor, and many require several. Each of the denominations or its publishing house
has information on its own publication (see list of publishing houses below). These publications (both national and regional) are also listed under the name of
the denomination in the *Yearbook of American and Canadian Churches,* published by Abingdon Press.

Book editors are also needed. Among these is the
editor-in-chief, or book director, who plans and supervises the program of the publishing house, solicits manuscripts from authors, and directs the work of the other
editors. These may be acquisitions editors, copyeditors,
and production editors. Their support staff includes
proofreaders and clerical workers. (See also opportunities for book editors in chapters 3 and 4.) Those
wishing to become book editors should take the same
type of journalism courses suggested for writers. Some
universities also offer special courses in book editing,
but most editors are trained on the job and through
workshops and other learning opportunities offered by

73

editorial and publishing associations (see the list at the close of this section).

Artists. Many artists and designers are needed in the publishing work of the churches. Much of this work is done free-lance and/or part time, but every publishing house maintains at least one full-time artist and designer in the production or editorial department. Training for these positions can be obtained in college art departments. There is also specialized training available in art schools.

Marketing Personnel. The books and magazines produced must of course be brought to the attention of and sold to those for whom they are intended, both churches and the general public. Thus there is a need in every publishing company for marketing personnel. This includes writers trained in advertising techniques, cataloguers, buyers, advertising agents, and the salespeople who call on the stores and other outlets to sell these books and materials. Special training in business techniques, sales, and advertising are valuable for any of the persons involved in these operations. There are many jobs available in these areas, and many engaged in sales have made a career of marketing religious materials for a denomination.

Bookstore Managers and Personnel. Church publishing houses also operate a number of bookstores that need managers and other personnel. Besides a general business background, these people should have a good knowledge of the book trade. The church-run stores tend to stock at least some general-interest books in order to provide a more complete service to their customers. Bookstore managers need to be aware of the curriculum that is being used in schools, the popular religious books (including paperbacks) that are being read, and should have a general appreciation of the message and ministry of the church groups represented in the store. (For a fuller explanation of this task, see chapter 3, Careers in Interdenominational and Interfaith Councils and Agencies.) Help in learning bookstore management is available from many sources; for information specifically about religious stores, contact the Christian Booksellers Association (CBA), 2031 West Cheyenne Road, Colorado Springs, CO 80906. Some idea of the extent of denominationally owned stores can be gained from realizing that there are more than sixty stores in the Southern Baptist chain and more than thirty Cokesbury (Methodist) stores.

Public Relations

Public relations is a vocation that has expanded phenomenally in churches and denominations in the last twenty-five years. Most denominations have departments that go under various titles such as communications, interpretation, publicity, or public relations. These departments employ many people who devote themselves to publicizing in the various media the programs and activities of the denomination.

The function of public relations workers can be briefly described as that of developing and maintaining public opinion favorable to the organization, its officers, its publications, and its pronouncements. In order to do this the workers must study the various media, know the persons involved in those media, understand the nature of the church and the message that they are to promote, and know the people involved in the church's operation. They are also cften called upon to provide materials for the use of churches and church members, the end result of which is to raise money for the program of the church and its mission at home and abroad.

There is need for both writers and publicists in performing these tasks. A number of news releases have to be written from time to time for distribution to the media. Some denominations maintain a news bureau whose job it is to write these releases, make arrangements for news conferences, and do the writing behind the scenes. In addition, staff are needed to keep contact with the media, interview the personnel of the church, and give help to church officers and leaders in how to best plan their activities to reach the greatest number of people.

A thorough knowledge of how the media operate is essential in public relations work; thus very often those workers who might have an interest in the mission of the church are recruited from newspapers and magazines.

Public relations workers should be trained in understanding people and their interests and needs. Often a public relations story will emphasize its human interest aspect, and it behooves a public relations person to know how to do this.

Public relations is a rapidly expanding field. Public relations people are needed not only in the national and regional offices of the churches, but full-time positions of this kind are available in many of the denominationally sponsored institutions of all kinds as well. For more information about this field, consult the denominational offices (see Appendix C) or for general information write to the Public Relations Society of America, 375 Park Avenue, New York, NY 10022; or the National Religious Publicity Council, 475 Riverside Drive, New York, NY 10027.

Radio and Television

Radio and television may be the fastest-growing area of career opportunities in religion today. The lion's share of jobs in this field are not under denomination sponsorship; therefore they are covered more thoroughly in chapter 4, Careers in Non–Church-Related Organizations.

However, some mention should be made of this career here, since the larger denominations are working in this area. In most cases the denomination's involvement in the media is under the sponsorship of the public relations or communications or interpretations office described previously. This may include preparing materials to be used in radio and television both to publicize the church's message to the general public and to train workers to interpret the church's message to its own members, including preparing materials to be used in the training of church leaders, volunteer workers, or fund solicitors.

College-trained persons with special skills and some experience and training are needed in this expanding field. An understanding of or experience in dramatics is often most valuable as is a knowledge of make-up, design, sound effects, and so forth. Short, intensive courses in radio and TV are arranged from time to time by denominations, colleges, seminaries and councils of churches. Because this is a somewhat new field, many have learned by doing after having had experience in other church work, religious education, journalism, or public relations.

Further information can be obtained from denominations (see Appendix C), from councils of churches with radio and TV departments, from the Director of Audio-Visual Communications of the National Council of Churches, 475 Riverside Drive, New York, NY 10027, or from such groups as The Protestant Radio and Television Center, Inc., 1727 Clinton Road NE, Atlanta, GA 30329.

For Further Information on Communications

In the whole area of communications much information is available. The following organizations can be very helpful:

The Protestant Church–Owned
Publishers Association
c/o Bob Boyd
127 Ninth Avenue North
Nashville, TN 37203

The Evangelical Press Association
P.O. Box 4550
Overland Park, KS 66204

The Associated Church Press
c/o Don Hetzler
P.O. Box 306
Geneva, IL 66134

It would also be useful to write to any of the following publishing operations run by denominations or their divisions:

Abingdon Press (Methodist) [1]
201 Eighth Avenue South
Nashville, TN 37203

Augsburg Publishing House (Lutheran)
426 South Fifth Street
Minneapolis, MN 55414

Beacon Press (Unitarian)
25 Beacon Street
Boston, MA 02108

Bethany Press (Christian Church)
Box 179 (2640 Pine Boulevard)
St. Louis, MO 63166

The Brethren Press (Church of the Brethren)
1451 Dundee Avenue
Elgin, IL 60120

Broadman Press (Southern Baptist)
127 Ninth Avenue North
Nashville, TN 37206

Concordia Publishing House (Lutheran)
3558 South Jefferson Avenue
St. Louis, MO 63118

---

[1] Retail sales are made through Cokesbury stores. Located throughout the U.S., these are retail outlets for United Methodist Church, United Presbyterian Church, and United Church of Christ and their publishing houses.

Faith and Life Press (Mennonite)
Box 347
724 Main Street
Newton, KS 67114

Fortress Press (Lutheran)
2900 Queen Lane
Philadelphia, PA 19129

Herald Press (Mennonite)
616 Walnut Avenue
Scottdale, PA 15683

John Knox Press (Presbyterian)
341 Ponce de Leon Avenue NE
Atlanta, GA 30308

Judson Press (American Baptist)
Valley Forge, PA 19481

Nazarene Publishing House
Box 527
Kansas City, MO 64141

Orbis Books (Catholic)
Maryknoll, NY 10545

Our Sunday Visitor Press (Catholic)
Noll Plaza
Box 920
Huntington, IN 46750

Paulist Press (Catholic)
1865 Broadway
New York, NY 10023

Seabury Press (Episcopal)
815 Second Avenue
New York, NY 10017

United Church Press, Pilgrim Press (United Church of
Christ)
287 Park Avenue South
New York, NY 10010

Warner Press (Church of God)
Box 2499
Anderson, IN 46011

Westminster Press (Presbyterian)
Witherspoon Building
Philadelphia, PA 19107

RELIGIOUS ORDERS

Anyone seriously considering a religious career will
want to investigate the possibility of becoming part of a
religious order. This idea may bring up visions of vows
of obedience and celibacy, and their accompanying existence in a closed community employed in menial
chores. Not so! Religious orders have changed, and
newer avenues are developing every day in a vast variety of occupations that are both challenging and
exciting.

One could almost say that every occupation listed in
this book is represented in some way in a religious
order. The only problem is to find the order that best
suits one's qualifications and talents and then become a
part of that community. Some of them require community living, but most do not.

The vast majority of religious orders are Roman
Catholic, but within them, what is offered in employment is very varied. Information can be obtained

through the diocesan office of vocations; this can be reached through any Catholic parish priest or church office. Or one can write to the National Conference of Diocesan Vocation Directors, PO Box 2086, Birmingham, AL 35201. Men interested in this avenue of careers can write to the National Conference of Religion Vocation Directors of Men, 22 West Monroe Street, Chicago, IL 60603. A very helpful guide entitled *A Guide for Men Interested in a Catholic Religious Vocation* is available free from SAC Vocation Information Center, PO Box 1930, Cherry Hill, NJ 08034. One of the best sources of information on Catholic orders for women is *The Directory of Religious Organizations* (Consortium Books, 1978).

Two indispensable guides to information about Catholic religious orders and what they offer in the way of religious careers have recently been published by Paulist Press. They are *Ministries for the Lord*, a resource guide and directory of Catholic Church vocations for men published in 1978, and *Images of Women in Mission*, a similar guide for women interested in church vocations published in 1979. These illustrated guides list alphabetically a hundred or more orders. For each order an explanation of its origins and history is provided, along with some idea of the type of work in which lay members of the order are involved. For each there are also addresses to which one can write for more information. The work of these orders both at home and abroad is covered in these books.

The Episcopal Church also offers opportunities for service through religious orders, though there are not nearly as many as in the Roman Catholic Church. *The Episcopal Church Annual*, published by Morehouse-Barlow, lists thirteen orders for men, sixteen orders for women, and one for men and women.

One avenue open to women in some churches is service through an order of deaconesses. This title dates back to biblical times, and as early as the third century there were deaconesses serving in the church; most were involved in caring for the sick. After the year 600 there is little mention of this office in the Roman Catholic Church. However, in the nineteenth century the office of deaconess was re-established in Germany by Lutheran institutions, and training schools were established there. It was at one of these that the famous Florence Nightingale, a wealthy English girl, received the training that she used as a nurse in the Crimean war. Deaconess training institutes were established in the United States, also by Lutheran Churches, mostly in connection with hospitals.

Deaconesses were formally employed in the Church of England and by British Methodists in the nineteenth century. As a result they came to America to serve in the Episcopal and Methodist churches, where they still continue to work.

Deaconesses are still serving in many capacities in Lutheran, Episcopal, and Methodist churches, and in a limited way in some other denominations. Their occupations include Director of Christian Education, church secretary, musician, parish visitor, and director of youth work. In settlement and community centers they serve as managers and program directors, kindergarten teachers, juvenile court workers, or social case workers. In hospitals they continue to have a place as nurses, dieticians, social workers, and in the many other occupations connected with similar kinds of institutions. They are also found in denominational and inter-denominational offices in various occupations.

Information on the work of deaconesses can be obtained from the following:

The Women's Division of Christian Service of the
United Methodist Church
475 Riverside Drive
New York, NY 10027

The National Center for the Diaconate (Episcopal)
1914 Orrington Avenue
Evanston, IL 60201

Lutheran Deaconess Association
Deaconess Hall
Valparaiso, IN 46383

Lutheran Deaconess Motherhouse
2224 West Kilbourn Avenue
Milwaukee, WI 53233

Information on many religious orders is also to be found in *The Directory of Religious Organizations*, a Consortium Book published by McGrath Publishing Co. (See also Appendix E for additional resources.)

SPECIALIZED MINISTRIES

In addition to all of these careers, which are common among churches, there are a host of other more specialized occupations which ought not be overlooked when considering a career under denominational sponsorship. These are occupations that are either so rare within denominations or so specialized that they are not common to all or most of them. The following are a few examples of what is available.

Historical Commissions

Every denomination and church group is in the process of recording its history and keeping archives. This is somewhat related to other occupations such as librarian or journalist, but it is quite a specialized craft, and one that takes special abilities and training. We will not attempt to list denominational historical commissions here since there are many, but most of them can be reached through the denominational headquarters (see Appendix C). In most cases they are not located in the headquarters building but are associated with a seminary or some other institution, such as the Presbyterian Historical Society, 425 Lombard Street, Philadelphia, PA 19147, which is one of the oldest and largest of these organizations. In most cases the historical commission of a denomination also publishes a quarterly or annual historical magazine and thus calls for writers and editors as well as archivists. A list of the main depositories of church historical material is found in the *Yearbook of American and Canadian Churches* (Abingdon Press).

Bible-Related Programs

Bible-related programs are covered in detail in chapter 3, Careers in Interdenominational and Interfaith Councils and Agencies, but as an example of a denominational operation let us mention here the Bible Reading Fellowship, Inc., P.O. Box M, Winter Park, FL

37290. This is a project of the Episcopal Church and is a U.S. representative of the Bible Reading Fellowship of England. This organization distributes daily Bible-reading notes, produces and distributes Bible study materials for individuals and groups, including cassettes and cassette study programs. It is a small operation, but one that serves a need in one particular church (although its materials are available to everyone) and represents another opportunity for a career in religion sponsored by a church body. There are similar groups in other churches which also should be studied for possible careers.

Renewal Services

Some of the renewal services, which are springing up all over the country, are covered in chapter 3, but we will mention here one such group in operation within the Catholic Church. It came into being because of the charismatic movement, which also exists in other denominations. Charismatic Renewal Services, P.O. Box 8617, Ann Arbor, MI 48107, is a "publishing company for magazines, books, tapes and music for the purpose of initiating, promoting and supporting the charismatic renewal in particular and Christian life in general within the Roman Catholic Church, and the whole Christian people in general." This group uses people in many different occupations: editors, secretaries, clerks, accountants, designers, marketing managers, data processers, sales representatives, cassette duplicators, music transcribers, and vocational counselors, to name a few. The company employs over one hundred people in this special ministry tied to the charismatic movement within the church, and it is representative of other such ministries that develop from time to time and employ people interested in religious careers of a special kind.

Lay Training and Activity

There are many groups within the borders of all the denominations that are involved in special lay activities, but one of the oldest and most active is a movement in the Lutheran Church–Missouri Synod, the Lutheran Layman's League, located at 2185 Hampton Avenue, St. Louis, MO 63139. This group began its specialized activity many years ago in support of a radio program that is still being broadcast on some one thousand eight hundred stations around the world, The Lutheran Hour. Later this group was expanded to a television ministry in the religious dramatic series, "This Is the Life." Beyond these two special ministries it has expanded its program to include many forms of worship, study, and evangelism, as well as the social services materials it provides. In addition it promotes retreats, workshops, rallies, and conferences to help Christians grow in faith and be witness to that faith in special ways. There are one hundred ten full-time employees engaged in many ways. The Layman's League operates almost entirely on free-will offerings from its members, but it is also an officially sponsored division of the Lutheran Church–Missouri Synod.

ADMINISTRATION

Among denominations, or national church bodies, there is need for a number of executives who administer the work of that denomination. These are the people working at the headquarters of a church body who are hired, usually by the board of the church, to administer its program and activities. All of these positions, whether elected or appointed, are involved in administrative duties. These are not entry-level positions, although some of the office jobs supervised by the executive may well be.

On almost every church board or division today (and it may go by another name), there is an executive and a staff to administer its program. Therefore the executives must have special training and experience in the particular division of the church that they are called upon to head, whether it be education, social welfare, or social action—or a board dealing with such things as pensions or church finances.

A person seeking a church-oriented career will probably want to consider, as well, employment in one of the church offices, either on a regional or national level. There are many such positions in every church and one can get information about the types and number of positions by writing to or visiting a denominational headquarters personnel office. In some cases the various divisions of a church body are not located in the same place. Many of these addresses are available at the end of this chapter and in Appendixes C and D.

LOCATIONS OF CHURCH HEADQUARTERS AND BOARDS

The following are the addresses of the major boards of the major bodies of Christians in the United States (those with memberships of more than one million). Information on smaller groups may be found in the

Yearbook of American and Canadian Churches, prepared annually by the National Council of Churches and published and distributed by the Abingdon Press.

When boards are located in more than one city or at different addresses, both addresses are given. Addresses of smaller boards and commissions may be obtained by writing to the main headquarters of the church body below.

Assemblies of God

International headquarters: 1445 Booneville Avenue, Springfield, MD 65802. All departments and offices of this church are located at the headquarters.

Baptists

American Baptist Churches in the USA. National offices of all boards are located at their headquarters: Valley Forge, PA 19481.

Southern Baptist Convention

Foreign Mission Board
3806 Monument Avenue
Richmond, VA 23230

Home Mission Board
1350 Spring Street
Atlanta, GA 30309

Sunday School Board (includes all publishing operations)
127 Ninth Avenue North
Nashville, TN 37234

Education and Christian Life Commissions
460 James Robertson Parkway
Nashville, TN 37219

Radio and Television Commission
6350 West Freeway
Fort Worth, TX 76116

Christian Church (Disciples of Christ)

Most major boards are located at the general offices:
222 South Downey Avenue
Box 1986
Indianapolis, IN 46206

Board of Publications
Box 179
2640 Pine
St. Louis, MO 63166

Board of Higher Education
119 North Jefferson
St. Louis, MO 63103

Episcopal Church

Headquarters of the executive council and national divisions are at 815 Second Avenue, New York, NY 10017.

Lutherans

American Lutheran Church.   422 South Fifth Street, Minneapolis, MN 55415. All boards and commissions are at this address.

Lutheran Church in America.   Most national boards are at headquarters address: 231 Madison Avenue, New York, NY 10016.

Boards of Education, Publication, Professional Services: 2900 Queen Lane, Philadelphia, PA 19129.

Lutheran Church–Missouri Synod.   Most national boards are at the headquarters: 500 North Broadway, St. Louis, MO 63102.

Publishing operations: 3558 Jefferson Avenue South, St. Louis, MO 63118.

United Methodist Church

Board of Church and Society
100 Maryland Avenue NE
Washington, DC 20002

Board of Discipleship (including education, evangelism worship, stewardship)
P.O. Box 840
Nashville, TN 37202

Board of Global Ministries (all ecumenical, health and welfare, relief, social concerns, national and world ministries)
475 Riverside Drive
New York, NY 10027

Board of Publication
United Methodist Publishing House
201 Eighth Avenue South
Nashville, TN 37202

Mormons

Church of Jesus Christ of Latter Day Saints. Headquarters and all national boards: 47 East South Temple Street, Salt Lake City, UT 84111

Orthodox

Greek Orthodox Archdiocese of North and South America. 8–10 East 79th Street, New York, NY 10021

Russian Orthodox Church in America. P.O. Box 675, Syosset, NY 11791

Presbyterians

Presbyterian Church in the U.S. All national boards are at headquarters address: 341 Ponce de Leon Avenue NE, Atlanta, GA 30308.

United Presbyterian Church U.S.A. All major boards under the two divisions of Program Agency and Vocation Agency are located at 475 Riverside Drive, New York, NY 10027. The publishing operation (Westminster Press) is located in the Witherspoon Building, Philadelphia, PA 19107.

Roman Catholic Church

Headquarters of the United States organization are under the National Conference of Catholic Bishops or the U.S. Catholic Conference, both at 1312 Massachusetts Avenue NW, Washington, DC 20005. This includes departments and divisions of education, communication, social development, education, family life, etc. Regional offices are located in the archdioceses and dioceses throughout the country.

United Church of Christ

Headquarters: 297 Park Avenue South, New York, NY 10010 (includes most boards)

Board of World Ministries: 475 Riverside Drive, New York, NY 10027

3

Careers in Interdenominational and Interfaith Councils and Agencies

Our survey of career opportunities in religion moves in ever-widening circles from the local church, to the denomination, to a look in this chapter at what is available in the councils and interdenominational agencies of the churches, and even in interfaith organizations.

These agencies and councils fall into some natural divisions. First there are the national groups, made up of church bodies of diverse backgrounds, such as the National Council of Churches of Christ in the USA and the National Association of Evangelicals. Then there are the regional groups, such as state or city councils of churches. These have been broadening their approach in recent years so that most of those that started out as Protestant councils, in most cases now include Roman Catholic churches and organizations, and many of them also have Jewish representatives, if not actual members. In addition, there are state or regional organizations of evangelical churches.

There are career opportunities as well in councils of faith groups such as the Lutheran Council in the USA supported by three national Lutheran bodies, or the Mennonite Central Committee, which unites the work of the several church bodies that call themselves by that name, and so on. There is also the World Council of Churches and corresponding international faith groups. These are treated in chapter 5, International Career Opportunities.

In addition, there are the groups that unite various denominations for a specific purpose, such as the Evangelical Church Library Association or the Protestant Radio and TV Center. Beyond these there are the interfaith organizations on various levels, such as the National Conference of Christians and Jews or the Church and Synagogue Library Association. All of these groupings offer employment opportunities.

Top level positions at interdenominational agencies tend to be filled by those who have had similar positions in denominational offices or programs. However, there are also many entry-level positions available in interchurch agencies as well.

COUNCILS OF NATIONAL CHURCH BODIES

The job opportunities in councils of national church bodies are similar to those in denominations: Each of the agencies has divisions of education, evangelism, health and welfare, social justice, stewardship, research, and the like, as well as offices of personnel and support services. For a description of the type of jobs available in the offices and field services of these councils see chapter 2, Careers in Church-Wide Institutions and Offices. However, on an interchurch or even interfaith level, the skills required are somewhat different, involving a greater knowledge of the backgrounds of the various churches that make up the council. Essentially, careers available here are those offered by two agencies: The National Council of Churches of Christ in the USA, with headquarters in the Inter-Church Center at 475 Riverside Drive, New York, NY 10027; and the National Association of Evangelicals at Box 28, Wheaton, IL 60187. The two organizations are similar in structure, but offer different career opportunities, both because of their theological complexion and the interest of the national churches that belong to each of them and plan and support their programs.

The National Council of Churches (NCC)

The NCC is the larger of the national interchurch agencies, and has the more diverse program. It is supported by thirty church bodies who hold official membership. These include most of the large churches except the Southern Baptists and some Lutherans. However, these denominations do participate in the program of the NCC through its various divisions and commissions.

The National Council of Churches came into being in 1950 as a successor to the old Federal Council of Churches and various other national groups which for many years had united the ecumenical endeavors of the churches. Its constitution reads as follows:

The National Council of the Churches of Christ in the United States of America is a cooperative agency of Christian communions seeking to fulfill the unity and mission to which God calls them. The member communions, responding to the gospel revealed in the Scriptures, confess Jesus, the incarnate Son of God as Saviour and Lord. Relying on the transforming power of the Holy Spirit, the Council works to bring churches into a life-giving fellowship and into common witness, study, and action to the glory of God and in service to all creation.

Under this broad purpose, the council is made up of a board of officers elected by the church, and the staff is elected or hired to carry out the mandates of the board and in turn of the member churches. There are three divisions of the program of the NCC: Church and Society, Education and Ministry, and Overseas Ministries. In addition, there are five commissions charged with specific responsibilities: Communication, Faith and Order, Regional and Local Ecumenism, Stewardship and Justice, Liberation and Human Fulfillment. In addition there are three offices: the Office of Research, Evaluation and Planning, the Office of Finance, and the Office of Personnel and Services.

Each of the divisions, commissions, and offices of the NCC has a staff of executives, assistants, and program directors, and a support staff of secretaries and maintenance workers. In each case the requirements for a career in any of these offices depend on the nature of the work and the program outlined by the officers of that division. The training and experience necessary to carry out these duties include an understanding of the churches that make up the membership and an ability to work with the people involved in each of the programs. Almost all of the offices listed below are located in the NCC headquarters in New York. Where there is another address, however, that is given separately.

A closer look at the job titles of the National Council of Churches reveals the very broad program that the council carries out and the great variety of talent required from its staff. In the office of general secretary there are three assistants: an associate general secretary, an executive assistant, and an executive director of the office on Christian-Jewish Relations. In addition, there is an assistant general secretary and associate director for the Washington office, located at 110 Maryland Avenue NW, Washington, DC 20002.

Under the division of Church and Society, the Associate General Secretary has staff associates for international affairs, religious and civil liberty, racial and ethnic concerns, economic concerns and social welfare, action and education, migrant field services, financial managements, worship and the arts, and a southeastern field representative. Related movements sponsored by this division include the Delta Ministry in the state of Mississippi, the Interfaith Center of Corporate Responsibility, the Inter-religious Foundation for Community Organization, and the National Farm Worker Ministries located on the West Coast and in the Midwest.

The second division of the NCC, Education and Ministry, also includes a variety of programs. Under the direction of the executive of this division there are three program areas. The first is education for Christian life and mission, and includes Friendship Press, the NCC's publishing division; sexuality and family ministries; public education issues, adult education, and leadership; special learning needs, vacation, leisure, and outdoor education; youth and adult mission education; and black Christian education resources. The second program involves education in society, including public education; and a united board for college development (159 Forrest Avenue NE, Atlanta, GA 30303), with divisions of academic administration, student services, and library administration. The third area concerns professional church leadership.

The third division of the NCC is the Division of Overseas Ministries, with functional officers located in the United States and geographic offices located around the world. Since the work of this division is concerned with overseas careers, information about it and its relationship to similar church boards is covered in chapter 5, International Career Opportunities.

As stated above, the NCC has five commissions. Their programs and personnel can be described as follows: (1) Communication Commission (general communications, broadcasting, broadcasting production, audio-visual communication, promotion and distribution, news and information, Ecumedia News Service, newspaper services and other special services; (2) Commission for Faith and Order (deals with theological issues); (3) Commission for Regional and Local Ecumenism (concerned with relationships with local and staff councils of churches and interfaith affairs); (4) Commission on Stewardship; (5) Commission on Justice, Liberation and Human Fulfillment.

In addition to these divisions and commissions of the NCC, there are the three already-mentioned offices that constitute the support staff of the council and its operations.

For further information about a career in the National Council of Churches, write to the directors of the respective offices described above, or to the Assistant General Secretary for personnel at 475 Riverside Drive, New York, NY 10027. In all there are 410 employees of the National Council of Churches of Christ in the USA.

National Association of Evangelicals

The NAE had its beginning in 1942, when one hundred fifty evangelical leaders met in St. Louis, Missouri, to launch a movement to bind together those local churches and national bodies that felt cooperation in a council of churches such as the NCC was compromising their more fundamental faith. Since then, the NAE has provided a means for this kind of "cooperation without compromise" among Bible-believing Christians. This fellowship is based on a statement of faith descriptive of the conservative evangelical Christian. The NAE represents thirty-five complete denominations (many very small), and has within its membership individual churches from at least twenty-eight other groups. Also included are Bible colleges, seminaries, ministerial fellowships, and evangelistic organizations, as well as individual Christians. Total membership in the NAE churches numbers above three million.

Through the ministries of its eight commissions and

five affiliated organizations, the NAE brings practical assistance to the churches. It is also active in speaking out, as advocate or opponent, on critical issues affecting evangelicals in legislation and national affairs. It carries on ministries through its commission and affiliates in such areas as evangelism, missions, education, world relief, and social concerns.

Although much younger than the NCC and its predecessor, the Federal Council of Churches, the NAE is a growing organization and represents many career possibilities for the person whose theological position is compatible with the strong conservative stand of this agency's member churches.

Organizationally the NAE consists of eight commissions (all located at its national headquarters at P.O. Box 28, Wheaton, IL 60187 unless otherwise indicated): Chaplaincy, Evangelical Churchmen, Social Action, Evangelism and Home Missions, Higher Education, Stewardship, Women's Fellowship, and World Relief; the last at P.O. Box 44, Valley Forge, PA 19481. In addition, it has five affiliates:

Evangelical Foreign Missions Association
1430 K Street NW
Washington, DC 20005

National Association of Christian Schools
P.O. Box 550
Wheaton, IL 60187

National Religious Broadcasters
Box 2544-R
Morristown, NJ 07960

National Sunday School Association
and
American Association of Evangelical Students
910 Elliot Avenue South
Minneapolis, MN 55404

Office of Public Affairs.   Located at 1430 K Street NW,
Washington, DC 20005, this office serves evangelicals
by monitoring pending legislation that may affect the
ministry of the churches or some spiritual issues. Assistance is also given to individuals, churches, and organizations in problems relating to the federal government.
There are six administrators on the staff.

Field Services.   Organizing and working with state and
local associations of evangelicals (there are twenty-four
regional and state associations in operation), the NAE
seeks to serve the local churches. Seminars on such
topics as church growth, stewardship, counseling, family life, and so on, are held regularly. There are four
administrative staff people involved.

Publications.   Numerous publications and news releases
flow out of the NAE office to keep evangelicals and the
religious community at large informed about programs
and issues of interest. A bimonthly publication, *Profile,*
and a quarterly magazine, *Action,* are published by this
department, with its four administrators and support
staff.

National Programs.   Periodically NAE coordinates programs with a nation-wide appeal. In 1976, for example,
NAE developed a program and materials for the bicen-

tennial year that were used by thousands of churches. Annually, materials are provided for the World Day of Prayer and seasonal Bible-reading programs. Staff is needed at the national headquarters to prepare these types of materials as well as plan the NAE national convention and one-day seminars held in various parts of the country.

Purchasing Service. Through this means, NAE provides equipment and supplies to churches, Christian workers, and missionaries at the lowest possible cost. The administrative staff numbers three.

Social Action. Through this commission, NAE serves as an educational medium on social needs. It coordinates the work of evangelical welfare organizations and encourages the application of biblical principles to the social needs of the day. It advises local groups in areas of social concerns and has helped establish child adoption agencies.

Christian Schools. Through the National Association of Christian Schools (an agency of NAE since 1947), the cause of Christian schools has been promoted. The group is moving toward forming a professional association of member schools and teachers.

National Religious Broadcasters. NRB has grown to well over five hundred member stations, program producers,and associates. This is a rapidly expanding field, and has been treated in chapter 2 in the section on Radio and TV careers. NRB has eight administrative staffs, plus support personnel.

World Relief. Active since the end of World War II, NAE's overseas relief arm has sent food and clothing worth many millions of dollars to needy people in all parts of the world. Work is coordinated through the missionaries and national church leaders overseas.

All of these constitute only a part of the program being carried on by this active association of evangelical churches, organizations, and individuals. The National Association of Evangelicals offers many career opportunities to interested individuals. Further information can be had from any of the addresses given above, the many state and regional associations, and the national headquarters.

REGIONAL COUNCILS OF CHURCHES

In every state and in most large cities, councils or federations of churches are formed to provide a basis for cooperative efforts and to give mutual support to the programs of churches in that community or region. The offices and staffs of these agencies provide hundreds of employment opportunities. In addition, there are regional and state councils of evangelical churches; these have sprung up more recently.

Neither type of council is a division of the large national bodies, the NCC or the NAE, but both have relationships with those bodies, and their programs and staff are a counterpart of the national groups. Each regional council, of course, reflects not only the origins, but also the membership of the larger organization.

Councils of Churches

In larger councils of churches one will usually find preponderantly main-line Protestant denominations, with a sprinkling of Catholic and sometimes Jewish members. The programs of these groups reflect a broad interest in the whole ministry of the church and its relationship to the community in which it finds itself. Thus the staff in these offices will be ecumenically-minded people acquainted with the whole church and its various facets and interests. Here one is apt to find staff interested (and involved) in social action, community improvement, health and welfare, and so on, in addition to the strictly religious activities of the churches.

The programs of these councils will vary according to location. The following is an outline of the staff of one city council which, while probably not typical, is at least representative of the kinds of activities councils are involved in, and the kind of training and preparation required for someone interested in a career in a local or state council of churches.

PERSONNEL CHART OF THE COUNCIL OF CHURCHES OF THE CITY OF NEW YORK

The New York City Council of Churches is one of the largest in the country (with an annual budget of $1.5 million), but its staff outline gives a picture of the type of careers available in city, state, and regional councils of churches.

105

Categories

In general, the staff positions (about 30) of the council can be divided into three categories: (1) program, with its primary function to carry out the program activities of the council; (2) administration, which deals with financial, budgetary, and administrative needs; and (3) clerical, which involves those positions that provide office supportive services.

Staff Titles

- Executive Director: duties include the primary administrative details of the council
- Director of Programs: duties include responsibility for all of the Council's programs
- Divisional directors for: church planning and research, communications (radio and TV), pastoral care, youth services, and the individual boroughs of Brooklyn, Manhattan, Staten Island, and the Bronx
- Comptroller, accounting staff, chaplain for chapel at Kennedy Airport, and group workers
- Nonprofessional, seasonal, part-time or full-time workers, including government contract workers, may be employed from time to time as needed
- Secretarial and clerical staff for each of the divisions and executives

For more information about what work is available and what is needed in this field, consult the local council of churches or interfaith council in any state or large city. Addresses are in the telephone directories. Sometimes the state council is coordinated with that of its largest city or the capital city.

Additional guidance can be obtained from the National Association of Council Secretaries, 475 Riverside Drive, New York, NY 10027, which was founded in 1940. This is an association of professional staff in ecumenical services throughout the country. It was established to provide creative relationships among these staffs and to encourage mutual support and personal and professional growth. This is accomplished by training programs, exchanges and discussions about concerns at conferences, and through the publication of a professional bimonthly journal, *On Location* (available from the National Association of Council Secretaries).

Evangelical Associations

As we mentioned, there are state and regional associations of evangelical churches. Some churches may hold membership in the local council of churches, but also feel the need for an association with other evangelicals. These councils are encouraged and given some support by the NAE, and are listed as affiliates in their annual reports. Information about these associations can be obtained from the local group or write to the National Association of Evangelicals, Box 28, Wheaton, Il 60187. The program of these evangelical associations and the requirements for staff are basically restricted to the spiritual ministry of the churches involved, and reflect the general character of the NAE itself.

Other Regional Groups

In addition to councils of churches and evangelical associations, in various parts of the country there may be associations of churches on a local, state, or regional basis. While they may have been formed for other purposes, in reality they have much the same type of ministry and program as the other councils. One such group is the Evangelistic Association of New England, 88 Tremont Street, Boston, MA 02108. This active organization, with a staff of executives, field workers, and support staff, carries on an extensive program involving churches throughout New England. Through seminars, conferences, publications, and deputation programs, this group provides leadership, training, and inspiration to both the clergy and laity of a wide variety of churches. It describes its ministries thus:

- Pastoral ministries: supportive groups designed for the encouragement and strengthening of the pastoral ministry
- Seminars: training in practical skills and living for Christian growth for both families and individuals
- Institutional ministries: bringing Jesus Christ to the hurt and lost in prisons, hospitals, and nursing homes
- Urban ministries: implementing and coordinating church development and Christian training in the city
- Church development and outreach: providing resource personnel to set up activities to help churches explore their full potential
- Communications services: creative communication resources and counsel for Christian organizations

- Information services: an information center to serve church leaders and concerned Christians

These are the kinds of exciting programs that are being conducted on an interchurch basis in many communities and regions. All of these need trained, skilled staff members, and thus offer many career opportunities.

COUNCILS OF NATIONAL FAITH GROUPS

Some denominational groupings made up of several national church bodies maintain national coordinating councils and offices for their faith groups. The career opportunities here are very similar to those of the denominations involved, most of which deal in those services to the churches and to the community that each of the bodies would be unable to provide individually, such as health and welfare, a news bureau—including radio and TV offices—campus ministries, theological studies, research and planning, government affairs, and the like. The following are major national coordinating offices and councils of such groups. Additional information can be obtained by writing to the addresses given.

Christian Holiness Association,
25 Beachway Drive, Indianapolis, IN 46224

This is the coordinating agency for those religious bodies that hold the Wesleyan Arminian theological view. It has twelve affiliated national bodies and six cooperating organizations.

Lutheran Council in the U.S.A.,
360 Park Avenue South, New York, NY 10010

A cooperative agency of the major American Lutheran Church bodies, its three objectives relate to the staff required: (1) to further the witness, work, and interests of the Lutheran Church; (2) to achieve theological concensus among Lutherans; and (3) to provide a means of cooperation and coordination of the efforts for a more effective and efficient service in six major areas: theological studies, education, mission, welfare, public relations, and service to military personnel. In addition to its New York headquarters, LCUSA maintains offices at 955 L'Enfant Plaza SW, Washington, DC 20024; and at 130 North Wells Street, Chicago, IL 60606.

Mennonite Central Committee,
21 South 12th Street, Akron, PA 17501

The relief and service agency of the North American Mennonite and Bretheren in Christ churches has representatives from seventeen Mennonite groups. MCC administers and participates in programs of agricultural and economic development, education, medicine, self-help, relief, peace, and disaster service.

North American Baptist Fellowship,
1628 Sixteenth Street NW, Washington, DC 20009

This is an organization of Baptist conventions in Canada, the United States, and Mexico, functioning as a regional body within the Baptist World Alliance to (1) promote fellowship among Baptists in North America, and (2) further the aims and objectives of the Baptist World Alliance so far as these affect the life of Baptist churches in North America. Membership includes nine national Baptist churches—most of the Baptist churches in North America.

Pentecostal Fellowship of North America, Keith at 25th NW, Cleveland, TN 37311

An agency of twenty-four national Pentecostal church bodies, it has the following objectives: (1) to provide a vehicle for expressing and coordinating efforts in matters common to all bodies, including missionary and evangelistic efforts; (2) to demonstrate the essential unity of spirit-baptized Christians; and (3) to provide services to its constituents to facilitate world evangelization and encourage the principles of community to nurture the church. The PFNA maintains local chapters and holds fellowship rallies for study and the exchange of views.

Standing Conference of Canonical Orthodox Bishops in the Americas, 8–10 East 79th Street, New York, NY 10021

Established to achieve cooperation among the various Eastern Orthodox Churches in the U.S., this agency centralizes and coordinates the mission of the church and acts as a clearing house for the church's efforts. Special departments are devoted to campus work, Christian education, military and other chaplaincies, and ecumenical relations.

SPECIALIZED INTERCHURCH AGENCIES

In addition to the organizations discussed, several cross-denominational agencies and councils have been organized to serve specific purposes. Each of these also offers some opportunities for careers in religion for those with the necessary skills. Some of these groups are listed below. Further information can be obtained by writing to them at the addresses given.

A Christian Ministry in the National Parks, 235 East 49th Street, New York, NY 10017

This ministry is an independent movement providing interdenominational religious services in fifty-five national parks, monuments, and recreation areas. Previously administered by the National Council of Churches, it became an independent movement in 1972. It represents more than forty denominations. Most of the staff members work part time because of the seasonal nature of this program. A good number of the positions of counselor and religious leader in each of the parks are open to unordained personnel.

Protestant Radio and Television Center, Inc. 727 Clifton Road NE, Atlanta, GA 30329

The PRTVC is an interdenominationally owned and operated institution concerned with Christian communications and humanistic values. Since its founding in 1949, the center has developed noncommercial communications programming of a religious, educational, cultural, and social service nature, using a variety of media: radio, TV, film, audio and video tape, photography, and print. Through seminars and workshops, PRTVC provides practical and theoretical training for clergy, teachers, and administrators of nonprofit organizations in the use of modern communication technology. The organization has thirteen employees involved in production—audio and video engineers and technicians, as well as administrators with skills in organizational management, program development, public relations, and fund-raising. As the communications field is burgeoning, this center reports a growing need for its services and personnel.

Lutheran Human Relations Association of America, Valparaiso University, Valparaiso, IN 46383

The LHRA group could be discussed elsewhere in this book, but since it combines the efforts of several national Lutheran church bodies in a particular activity, it belongs in the category of a specialized interchurch agency. This association's stated purpose is "seeking to equip Christians to alleviate, and when possible overcome, racism, sexism, and other forms of injustice." Although it is small, it is typical of other organizations dealing with social justice issues on either a church or interchurch basis. Its program includes publications, workshops conducted in congregations and regional associations of churches, and other attempts to use the existing church media for promoting its purposes. LHRA also provides resource persons to churches and agencies as needed. Prospective employees are expected to have college and some graduate training, a grounding in Lutheran theological principles, and a basic knowledge of current social justice issues.

Federation of Protestant Welfare Agencies, Inc., 281 Park Avenue South, New York, NY 10010

This federation is typical of many in large American cities: It unites the services of church-owned welfare agencies. Since this one is in the largest city in the U.S., it serves as consultant for, and ties together the activities of, more than three hundred agencies in the social and health fields located chiefly in the New York City area. Although the agency itself has a small staff, and the member agencies do their own hiring, the Federation is a source of information about career opportunities in the field in New York, and can direct the inquirer to its member agencies for more information. In addition to the many welfare activities of the Federation, it also offers to provide agencies with help in finding executives and other staff. In addition, it has an accredited training program for staffs of its member agencies.

Press and Publishing Associations

There are three major press associations binding together the religious magazines and newspapers published in the United States. All of them are small organizations with little opportunity for religious careers in themselves. However, we mention them here as one of the sources of information about interdenominational careers in religious journalism. A more complete description of the careers available is found in chapter 2, Careers in Church-Wide Institutions and Offices, and chapter 4, Careers in Non–Church-Related Organizations. For information about these associations, consult any of the following. They are in touch with their members.

Evangelical Press Association, Inc.
P.O. Box 4550
Overland Park, KS 66204

Associated Church Press
P.O. Box 306
Geneva, IL 66134

Catholic Press Association
119 North Park Avenue
Rockville Center, NY 11570

Similarly, there are publishers' associations that are sources of information about publishing. In the interdenominational category, the best source of help is the Protestant Church-Owned Publishers Association, 127 Ninth Avenue North, Nashville, TN 37203.

Church Women United in the U.S.A., Room 812, 475 Riverside Drive, New York, NY 10027

CWU is an ecumenical lay movement providing Protestant, Orthodox, and Roman Catholic women with programs for and access to involvement in church, civic, and national affairs. CWU has some two thousand units formally organized in communities located in all fifty states and the District of Columbia. CWU employs ten staff persons, their assistants, and support personnel in the areas of citizen action, communications, community services, ecumenical relations, financial management, legislative affairs, urban ministries, as United Nations consultants, and in the direction of local and state units of CWU. It also publishes a periodical, *The Church Woman.*

115

INTERFAITH ORGANIZATIONS

In the ever-widening circle of career opportunities in religion, one also ought to consider interfaith organizations. The dialogue between Catholics and Protestants has been going on at several levels for a long time, with some encouraging results. Relations between these two groups has improved. Similarly, the dialogue between Christians and Jews is a part of the religious scene in America and provides another opportunity for religious careers.

National Conference of Christians and Jews, 43 West 57th Street, New York, NY 10019

The NCCJ is one of the oldest and most effective of the interfaith groups. It is a nonprofit human relations organization engaged in a nation-wide program of inter-group education to eliminate prejudice and discrimination. Founded in 1928, the NCCJ states that its purposes are:

> ... to build bridges of understanding among all groups, to bring the forces of enlightenment and education to bear upon racial and religious prejudice, and to achieve implementation of the moral law; giving others the same right and respect we desire for ourselves. It enlists all those who, without compromise of conscience or of their distinctive commitments, work to build better relationships among persons of all religions, races and nationalities.

The NCCJ is engaged in this program on several fronts and therefore needs knowledgeable, able persons for its work. It conducts seminars and conferences of various kinds each year, in line with the purposes stated above. An example of this is the annual conference, first held in 1970, on the "Church Struggle and the Holocaust." Here, Christian and Jews, clergy and laity meet to examine the Nazi persecutions and to draw lessons for the future so that there will be mutual understanding and resistance to prejudice. In a like vein, the NCCJ has put together a book of suggestions for Christian congregations that wish to observe an annual Christian Service of Holocaust Remembrance. The writing of these materials and the conducting of these programs are examples of the work of NCCJ staff.

In addition to the many programs that the NCCJ sponsors, it also owns and operates the Religious News Service, which furnishes news of religious events and happenings in all faiths to subscriber papers and magazines. This operation has a constant need for religious journalists. They work out of the New York office, but many also serve as "stringers" or correspondents in all parts of the country.

For information about a career in the National Conference of Christians and Jews or the Religious News Service, write either organization.

Church and Synagogue Library Association, P.O. Box 1130, Bryn Mawr, PA 19010

The CSLA is concerned primarily with libraries in local congregations, but also acts as a clearing house between library associations of various denominations, such as the Catholic Library Association and the Association of Jewish Libraries. CSLA can give information to those interested in religious library careers at all levels.

For Further Information

For more information and help in any area of finding or developing a career in interchurch or interfaith areas, write the Office for Professional Church Leadership at the National Council of Churches, 475 Riverside Drive, Room 770, New York, NY 10027. The Council also produces a packet of materials for use by individuals considering church careers or by career counselors. Included in this packet are brochures such as those entitled, "What is a Church Occupation?" and "A Listing of Church Occupations."

In addition, the Council's office acts as a clearing house for the Church Career Development Council, which has approved and accredited the fourteen centers where further counseling on careers is available. (See Appendix D for a complete list of these centers and their addresses.)

4

Careers in Non-Church-Related Organizations

One of the largest and most rapidly growing fields for religious careers is in non–church-related religious organizations and institutions. We will attempt to survey that field in this chapter, although a complete overview is impossible because the organizations and also the work opportunities change so quickly here.

Most of these organizations are comparatively recent in origin. Some of them are very new, and no doubt a number of others will have come on the scene while this book is going to press. Many non–church-related agencies are very large: Campus Crusade for Christ International, for instance, has hundreds of locations all over the world and employs upwards of six thousand persons in a multitude of occupations. Other groups are very small, such as the John Milton Society for the Blind, an important ministry that employs very few people.

How many of these organizations there are, is hard to determine because of the fluid nature of the various movements that bring them into being. Intercristo, the International Christian Organization in Seattle, Washington, is set up to deal with the employment problems of these organizations. At least once a year, it lists nearly six hundred agencies of the type we are dealing with in this chapter in their *Directory of Christian Work Opportunities.* In addition to publishing this index, Intercristo provides personal counseling services to individuals and groups interested in finding employment in religious occupations. For a full explanation, write or call (toll-free): Intercristo, Box 9323, Seattle, WA 98109, tel: (800)426–0507.

Many of the organizations listed by Intercristo offer only or primarily overseas work opportunities. We will discuss these in more detail in chapter 5, International Career Opportunities.

In this chapter we will survey the career opportunities available in organizations whose work is primarily in the United States. We have broken them down into seven major categories: (1) evangelism (including that conducted among youth); (2) educational operations (schools, colleges, and other training institutions); (3) Bible societies, including the work of translation and distribution of the Scriptures; (4) publishing, including the writing and production stages, as well as the selling operations connected with books, magazines, and other periodicals; (5) radio and television ministries; (6) outdoor activities such as camps and retreat centers; and (7) specialized services to certain groups.

What kinds of careers are available in the organizations dealing primarily with religious affairs but not related to any church or church group? These are almost as varied as the list of jobs at any typical employment agency. One can get an idea of the varied character of employment opportunities in religious organizations by looking at the following alphabetical list from Intercristo's *Directory of Christian Work Opportunities* (remember that these are only the *actual openings* available at the time this large book was printed):

Job Classifications

Accounting
Administration
Administration, Camp
Advertising
Agriculture
Air Traffic Control
Aircraft Pilot/Instructor
Anaesthesiology
Animal Husbandry
Anthropology
Archery Instruction, Camp
Architecture
Aviation Mechanics
Bible School Education
   Administration
   Christian Ed
   English-Journalism
   French
   General
   Hebrew
   Lib-Info Sci
   Music
   Theology-Bible

Bookkeeping
Bookkeeping, Camp
Bookstore/Management
Building/Contracting
Bus/Truck Driving
Business Management, Camp
Camp Counseling
Cardiology
Carpentry
Cassette Prod/Duplication
Chemistry
Child Evangelism
Childcare
Christian Education
Church Planning/
   Development
Cinematography
Clerical Work/Typing
College-Univ Education
   Administration
   Art Business Ed
   Counseling
   English-Journalism

General
Home Economics
Lib-Info Sci
Math
Music
Physical Ed
Science
Social Science
Speech
Theology-Bible
Communications Research
Community Development
Cooking
Cooking/Food Service Mgt.,
   Camp
Corrections/Penal Work
Corres Course Writing/
   Counseling
Counseling
Counselor Training, Camp
Crafts Instruction, Camp
Curriculum Writing/Editing
Data Entry
Dental Hygiene
Dental Technology
Dentistry
Dermatology
Discipleship Ministry
Drafting
Drama Instruction, Camp
Drama/Theatre Arts
Editing, Print Media
   Management
   Programming
   Systems Analysis
Electrical Work

Electronics
Elementary Education
   Administration
   Christian Ed
   English-Journalism
   General
   Lib-Info Sci
   Math
   Music
   Physical Ed
   Science
   Spanish
   Special Ed
   Speech
   Theology-Bible
Emergency Relief
Engineering
   Agricultural
   Architectural
   Chemical
   Civil
   Electrical
   Environmental
   Industrial
   Mechanical
   Mining/Petroleum
   Other
English Teaching/Second
   Lang
Estate Planning
Ethnomusicology
Evangelism
Evangelism Follow-Up
Field Communications
Film Production
Financial Control

Financial Development
Food Service
  Management
  Work
  Work, Camp
Forestry
Graphic Arts
Gymnastics Instruction,
    Camp
Heavy Construction
Heavy Equipment Operation
Helicopter Pilot/Instructor
Horsemanship Instructor,
    Camp
Hospital Administration
Hospitality
Houseparent
Indian Lore Instruction,
    Camp
Internal Medicine
Journalism
Lawyer
Linguistic Analysis/Research
Literacy Work
Literature Distribution/Sales
Maintenance
Maintenance, Camp
Marketing/Sales
Masonry
Mechanics
Medical
  Instruction
  Records Admin
  Technology
Metal Work
Midwifery

Music
  Arranging/Conducting
  Instruction, Camp
  Ministry
  Instrumental
  Keyboard
  Vocal/Choral
Nature Instruction, Camp
Nurses Aide
Nursing, Camp
Nursing, Practical
Nursing, Registered
Nutrition/Dietetics
Obstetrics/Gynecology
Occupational Therapy
Office Work, General
Ophthalmology
Optometry/Lens Mfg
Otolaryngology, ENT
Outdoor Crafts Instr, Camp
Painting
Paramedical Work
Pastorate, Assistant
Pastorate, Senior
Pediatrics
Personal Evangelism
Personnel
Pharmacy
Photography
Photography Instruction,
    Camp
Physical Therapy
Physician, General Medicine
Pioneer Missions Work
Plumbing
Pre-school Ed/Christian Ed

Pre-school Ed/General
Printing
Program Administration,
    Camp
Psychology
Public Health Work
Public Relations
Purchasing
Radio Engineering
Radio Programming
Radio/TV
    Announcing
    Copywriting
    News Reporting
    Time Sales
Radiology
Riflery Instruction, Camp
Scientific Research
Secondary Education
    Administration
    Art
    Business Ed
    Christian Ed
    Counseling
    Engineering
    English-Journalism
    French
    General
    German
    History
    Home Economics
    Lib-Info Sci
    Manual Arts
    Math
    Music
    Physical Ed

Science
Social Science
Spanish
Special Ed
Speech
Theology-Bible
Secretarial Work
    Camp
    Executive
    Medical
Seminary Education
    Christian Ed
    General
    Greek
    Lib-Info Sci
    Music
    Theology-Bible
Servicemen's Work
Social Work
Sports Supervision, Camp
Statistics
Street Evangelism
Student Evangelism
Surgery
Tchr Training
Team Evangelism
Theol Ed by Extension
Toolmaking
Translation
TV Camera Operation
TV Engineering
TV Programming
Veterinary Medicine
Voc-Indus Education
    Administration
    Art

Business Ed	Water Sports/Boating
General	Women's Work
Manual Arts	Writing
Special Ed	X-Ray Technology
Speech	Youth Ministry

The total number of positions available is rather astounding also. Again, these are only actual openings at the time Intercristo's directory was printed. Jobs are grouped into the ten categories Intercristo has developed for its index, but under each there is great variety, as we have seen. The following list shows the number of jobs listed at the time the 1979 directory was put together:

Church/Evangelism	900
Business/Data Processing	648
Camping	480
Education	792
Mass Communication/Fine Arts	360
Medicine	480
Science/Technology	108
Social Services	240
Support Services	360
Translation/Linguistics	120

There were thus a total of 4,488 listings at the time of publication. Also, since each of these listings represents four to five openings, this means there were some twenty thousand openings in all. And since there are relatively few of the totals listed, the actual employees in each organization must be a very large number. Even discounting the fact that some of these are overseas jobs and some are seasonal (such as those in camping), it is still a large number. And one must remember that although Intercristo deals with many organizations, there are many other groups that do not use its services.

Let's take a close look, then, at what is available in terms of careers in these organizations.

EVANGELISM

Some of the largest religious organizations in the world are involved in the various activities that come under the broad classification of evangelism, and they offer many opportunities for careers in religion.

Some of these organizations carry the names of their founders or of top evangelists, such as the Billy Graham Evangelistic Association located in Minneapolis, the Oral Roberts organization in Tulsa, or the Morris Cerullo world evangelism operation in San Diego. These and other organizations like them are primarily involved in staging evangelistic "campaigns," which last for a week, more or less, in a city or other large center, but the planning and preparatory work plus the follow-up involve hundreds of people in a wide variety of pursuits—writers, publicists, radio and TV specialists, as well as the support staff of the headquarters operation. The Billy Graham Evangelistic Association, for example, employs four hundred people in its office in Minneapolis. These persons represent the full range of office workers, from file clerks to the most sophisticated of computer operators.

On location where the campaigns are held, there is a need for hundreds of persons as well—not only the theologically trained evangelists staff and workers, but the musicians, the technicians, and the many others who make these operations so well-run and effective.

Several of the largest of the religious organizations concerned primarily with evangelism concentrate on work with youth. The best known of these perhaps are Youth for Christ, with its headquarters in Wheaton, Illinois; Young Life, in Colorado Springs, Colorado; and Campus Crusade for Christ International, in San Bernardino, California. Each of these large groups plus many smaller ones need staff people and are actively recruiting workers who will dedicate themselves to a career in evangelism.

Campus Crusade for Christ International, Arrowhead Springs, San Bernardino, CA 92414.

For our purpose here, in order to show the type of work involved, the kinds of persons needed, and the training suggested and available, we will look at Campus Crusade for Christ in detail. A similar study could be made of each of the other organizations we have mentioned; for more information, contact the personnel director at the addresses given at the close of this section.

Campus Crusade was founded in 1951 as a ministry to students at UCLA. From this modest beginning has developed a group still committed primarily to work with high school and college students, but embracing a ministry that employs thousands of staff members around the world. In 1979 it had 6,400 employees, of which about 4,000 are in the United States. With a variety of ministries within the program, Campus Crusade can use persons in almost every imaginable profession. The vast majority are unordained.

Campus Crusade reaches into every segment of society. Some employees work in colleges, high schools, military installations, communities, and churches around the world. Others are using their professional skills and training as secretaries, electricians, accountants, carpenters, doctors, teachers, artists, writers, and businessmen, to name but a few of the professions involved.

Campus Crusade, in its literature to prospective employees, lists occupation possibilities in the field and at its headquarters.

In the Field. This is the area in which the greatest number of workers are involved in a variety of ministries. The Campus Ministry challenges the college community with the claims of Christ through weekly training meetings, evangelistic outreach, prayer groups, Bible studies, and sessions with faculty, civic leaders, and local churches. The High School Ministry is similar to the Campus Ministry, but operates on the high school level. The Lay Ministry works with pastors and church leaders to develop strategies for reaching entire communities and cities, and to train the laity in evangelism efforts. The International Ministries reach students from other countries who are studying in the United States; they also assist the national staff overseas. The Military Ministry works in close cooperation with chaplains. These persons work with enlisted men, officers, reserves, National Guard, their dependents, and retired military personnel. The Agape Movement is primarily an international operation, a kind of Christian peace corps. This will be treated more thoroughly in chapter 5, International Career Opportunities. In the Athletic Ministry, both amateurs and professionals involved in six major sports work among their fellow teammates. The work ranges from sharing on a one-to-one basis to presenting Christ to tens of thousands at the Olympic Games. The International Students Ministry helps to reach the thousands of foreign students studying in the U.S., and trains them to present Christ to their own people when they return home. The Intercultural Ministry is concerned with American minorities: native Americans, blacks, Hispanics, Asian Americans, and others. Campus Crusade's Great Commission Prayer Crusade challenges and involves men and women of all ages. In the Prison Ministry, many personnel are involved in working with institutions throughout the U.S. and Canada and with parolees and their families in adjusting to society. The Camping Ministry trains college students who work in Christian camps of all types in the summer months. Music Ministry staff members are involved in musical groups, performing in churches, civic organizations, military installations, prisons, high schools, and colleges throughout the U.S. and the world.

At the Headquarters. The international headquarters of Campus Crusade coordinates the overall planning and operation for the entire ministry described above. Located at Arrowhead Springs, California, the offices and guest accommodations are in what was formerly a luxury hotel nestled in the mountains overlooking the San Bernardino Valley. Hundreds of staff members are involved in the heartbeat of this international organization. Any group with more than six thousand persons on its staff needs experienced men and women to plan, program, coordinate, write, type, file, and keep the books. The Campus Crusade offices include a variety of departments. The conference services involve the conference facilities of the headquarters. These are in constant use by groups and individuals, and the staff required is comparable to that of a modern hotel. The personnel department is responsible for recruiting and placing men and women in the Campus Crusade operation around the world. The administration of all the financial policies and management of the business end of Campus Crusade are run by the accounting department. In the mass media department, writers, artists, printers, and photographers create and produce a variety of periodicals, brochures, pamphlets, and posters needed by the staff. This department also includes public relations people, and runs a news bureau. Audio-visual staff develop tools for use in evangelism. The radio-TV staff is responsible for producing TV specials and spots for radio use. Staff lawyers in the legal department serve as counsels to the corporation on all legal matters. The marketing department is concerned with bringing to the general public the materials produced by Campus Crusade and others. Donor relations staff members maintain personal communication with individuals who are committed to financial support of the work of Campus Crusade. The workers in computer services coordinate the activities, and accelerate and raise the efficiency of the world-wide ministry. The mail systems is a conglomerate of departments dealing both with the thousands of daily incoming letters and with the correspondence carried on by the staff. Through the direct mail department, individuals and organizations are motivated to become involved in the world-wide activities of Campus Crusade's various ministries.

One interested in working with an organization like Campus Crusade may well ask what kind of person is needed for the staff positions, what the job qualifications are. To answer these questions, Campus Crusade has prepared the following statement. Its requirements are typical of those for the staff of any of the many religious organizations working in the field of evangelism.

"Standards for Staff: Underlying every standard for staff are two spiritual qualifications: a heart for God and a teachable attitude. No physical requirements are as important.

"The following guidelines are designed as much for a potential staff member's personal assessment as for our own.

"1. Spiritual Maturity—Emphasis is placed on the quality of spiritual life. Each applicant must understand and be in full accord with the Campus Crusade for Christ Statement of Faith and with our emphasis on the ministry of the Holy Spirit. Each applicant must show evidence of walking by faith and there should be a good growth pattern in prayer and Bible study habits. Each applicant must have been a Christian for at least one year before beginning an active ministry with Campus Crusade.

"2. Calling—Each applicant must be able to state clearly why he believes that God is leading him into the Campus Crusade for Christ ministry.

"3. Effectiveness of Witness—Each applicant must show concern for others and evidence of past fruitfulness. If there is a concern without fruitfulness, there must be manifested a willingness to learn how to introduce others to Christ.

"4. Knowledge of Scripture—Campus Crusade places a strong emphasis on Scripture and its application to daily life. In addition to this basic knowledge of Scripture, every applicant is also expected to attend the Institute of Biblical Studies Training Program.

"5. Personality and Character—Each applicant should have leadership potential and be attractive to others in both personality and character. Priority is placed on dependability, willingness to assume responsibility and a teachable spirit.

"6. Emotional Stability—Each applicant must be emotionally stable. This is determined by psychological questionnaires, application material and the opinion of the interviewing group.

"7. Academic Training—Staff applicants must have either the necessary formal education or on-the-job training to meet the demands of his assignment. In the case of non-college graduates, the judgment will be made by an evaluation committee especially for those skilled as electricians, printers, plumbers, musicians, secretaries, etc. A college degree is essential for those working on the university campus or with high school students.

"8. Personal Appearance—Applicants must be neat, well-groomed and willing to dress appropriately for their assignment.

"9. Physical Qualifications—Each applicant must submit a standard health form which has been completed by a qualified physician. Due to the nature of this ministry, handicaps may prevent an individual from qualifying for staff; however, exceptions are considered.

"10. Training—Staff members in the United States are expected to attend Staff Training annually.

"11. Tenure—All applicants are encouraged to consider this a lifetime ministry. But all are expected to spend not less than two years in the ministry, assuming there is mutual agreement."

For further information about career opportunities with Campus Crusade for Christ International, write to the Director of Personnel, Arrowhead Springs, San Bernadino, CA 92414.

For purposes of comparison and to demonstrate the variety of career opportunities in different types of religious groups engaged in evangelism, let us look at some of these opportunities. Many of the needs of and requirements for programs would be the same as for Campus Crusade, but there are some differences to be noted. (Further information can be obtained by writing to any of the organizations involved.)

Billy Graham Evangelistic Association
1300 Harmon Place, Minneapolis, MN 55403

Perhaps the best known evangelical organization, both because of the extent of its work as well as the large television coverage in the past few years, the Billy Graham Evangelistic Association should be surveyed for career opportunities. Most of the activity of this association is connected with its huge campaigns throughout the world, for which there is very extensive advance planning and organization. In addition, the home office staff numbers four hundred. Much of this staff is concerned with the extensive mail load, the publication of *Decision* magazine and other promotional materials, and the financial work of the organization.

Christian Service Brigade, Inc.,
P.O. Box 150, 380 Schmale Road, Wheaton, IL 60187

The Christian Service Brigade is a nonprofit church-service organization with representatives located through the U.S. The focus of its ministry is reaching men and boys via a Christ-centered program carried out through the churches. Its sixty employees are engaged as field representatives; as writers, editors, and artists for curriculum materials; and as a support staff of managers and office personnel.

High School Evangelism Fellowship, Inc., 10 Garber Square, Ridgewood, NJ 07450

Describing its purpose as "world-wide evangelization of high school students and the Scriptural training of Christian students in the principles of Christian living and witnessing," the High School Evangelism Fellowship has twenty-seven full-time employees and other part-time or volunteer leaders of clubs throughout the country.

Inter-Varsity Christian Fellowship, 233 Langdon Street, Madison, WI 53703

The Inter-Varsity Christian Fellowship is a large, well-known organization that has been active for many years on college campuses. It describes its purpose as follows: "To establish, assist and encourage colleges, universities, nursing schools and other comparable education institutions in the U.S.A., groups of students (and faculty members) who witness to the Lord Jesus Christ as God Incarnate and have three major objectives: evangelism, discipleship, and missions." Inter-Varsity also publishes periodicals and books. It employs two hundred fifty in the field, and another two hundred in the national office and the literature department.

134

Pioneer Girls, Inc., Box 788, Wheaton, IL 60187

Pioneer Girls is a counterpart to the Christian Service Brigade, but it ministers to girls and women. It has a club and a camping program for which it produces its own curriculum. Its purpose is described as "a Bible-based, Christ-centered girls' program that results in personal growth for the girl in her total life and prepares her for Christian service." Pioneer girls has twenty-one employees as well as some additional staff for camps and other seasonal and part-time activities.

Youth for Christ International
Box 419, Wheaton, IL 60187

Youth for Christ has a varied program of activities, including Campus Life clubs in high schools, in addition to neighborhood ministries for those in disadvantaged situations, group homes for institutional care of youth, and a variety of counseling and referral services. YFC is at work in 1,100 communities in the U.S. and in 52 countries. It employs 800 full-time and 3,800 part-time and volunteer workers.

In addition to the above, persons interested in this type of career should examine the following list of other organizations engaged primarily in evangelistic endeavors. For information write to the organization's personnel director.

Child Evangelism Fellowship
44 Ionia S.W.
Grand Rapids, MI 49501

Christian Businessmen's Committee
P.O. Box 3380
Chattanooga, TN 37404

Family Concern
1415 Hill Avenue, Box 207
Wheaton, IL 60187

Fellowship of Christian Athletes
8701 Leeds Road
Kansas City, MO 64129

Full Gospel Business Men's Fellowship
836 South Figueroa Street
Los Angeles, CA 90017

International Gospel League
854 East Washington Boulevard
Pasadena, CA 91102

Morris Cerullo World Evangelism
P.O. Box 700
San Diego, CA 92138

Oral Roberts
777 South Lewis
Tulsa, OK 74105

Rural Bible Mission
5325 West F Ave.
Kalamazoo, MI 49009

EDUCATION

There are many opportunities for a teaching career in religious institutions. A detailed discussion of this career is found in chapter 2, in the section on education. Since teaching in a religious college is similar in most respects to that in other institutions of higher education, the preparation, training, and requirements in most disciplines are exactly the same as those in secular institutions. Therefore the most comprehensive information on college teaching is to be found in other books on education careers.

Nevertheless, there are areas of concern for teachers in religious colleges that differ from those in other institutions. If one is considering a career in a religious institution, these areas should be investigated. For further information, write to:

The Council of Protestant Colleges and Universities
1818 R Street NW
Washington, DC 10036

The Commission on Higher Education of the National Council of Churches
475 Riverside Drive
New York, NY 10027

Department of Higher Education of the U.S. Catholic Conference
1312 Massachusetts Avenue NW
Washington, DC 20005

If one is considering teaching or working in a college with an evangelical emphasis, the following colleges are members of the National Association of Evangelicals:

John Brown University
Siloam Springs, AR 72761

Azusa Pacific College
Highway 66 at Citrus
    Avenue
Azusa, CA 91702

Biola College
13800 Biola Avenue
La Mirada, CA 90639

Christian Heritage College
2100 Greenfield Drive
El Cajon, CA 92021

Pasadena College
1539 East Howard Street
Pasadena, CA 91004

Westmont College
955 La Paz Road
Santa Barbara, CA 93108

Rockmont College
8801 West Alameda Avenue
Denver, CO 80226

Clearwater Christian College
3400 Gulf to Bay
Clearwater, FL 35515

Trinity Christian College
P.O. Box 565
Palos Heights, IL 60463

Wheaton College
501 East Seminary
Wheaton, IL 60187

Taylor University
Upland, IN 46989

Asbury College
Wilmore, KY 40390

Gordon College
Wenham, MA 01984

John Wesley College
1020 South Washington
    Street
Owosso, MI 48867

The King's College
Briarcliff Manor, NY 10510

Cedarville College
Cedarville, OH 54314

Oral Roberts University
777 South Lewis
Tulsa, OK 74105

Barrington College
Middle Highway
Barrington, RI 02806

Bob Jones University
Greenville, SC 29614

Bryan College   LeTourneau College
Bryan Hill   P.O. Box 7001
Daton, TN 37321   Longview, TX 75601

Bible Colleges

The general classification Bible colleges are to schools whose academic level is different than that of most colleges. The concentration in these post–high-school institutions is on the study of the Bible both as a discipline in itself and as it relates to other areas of life. Most of these institutions also offer courses of training in religious work so that their graduates may be better fitted for employment in a religious institution or as a secretary or parish worker in a local church. Many graduates go on to complete their education in accredited colleges.

Some Bible schools were founded originally by persons of one denomination. The majority, however, were founded and are still run by independent groups whose theological stance is evangelical.

One of the largest of these schools is the Moody Bible Institute in Chicago. It will serve as an example of the type of career possibilities available in such institutions. Moody has an extensive publishing operation; this will be discussed under "Publishing," in this chapter. The Moody Bible Institute also has its own radio station. But primarily it is a school for the training of the laity in the Bible. It has a large student body and an active program, and thus employs some six hundred full-time people in about two hundred different jobs: editors, writers, teachers, computer technicians, radio broadcasting personnel, food service operators, maintenance engineers, secretaries, clerks, graphic artists, printers, accountants, and so on. Persons interested in this school should write to the Department of Personnel, Moody Bible Institute, 820 North La Salle Street, Chicago, IL 60610.

The National Association of Evangelicals lists seventy-five accredited Bible colleges. This list and further information can be obtained from the American Association of Bible Colleges, Box 543, Wheaton, IL 60187.

Specialty Training Institutes

In addition to colleges and Bible institutes, there are many different types of specialty training institutions around the country that have Christian, but not necessarily church, sponsorship. One such school is the Narramore Christian Foundation (Box 5000, Rosemead, CA 91770). It specializes in training people for Christian counseling, and holds frequent one-week seminars for business and professional people. The purpose of these seminars is to help the participants gain insight through psychological tests and classes in order to become more effective in their work. In addition, twice each year there are three-week intensive counseling training sessions. These attract ministers and missionaries, chaplains and deans of colleges, and others whose daily work involves counseling. Instructors are Christian psychologists, counselors, and others on the professional staff. The Narramore Institute also has a daily radio show that is broadcast on 170 stations throughout the U.S. and overseas, a literature publishing ministry in the counseling field, and a missionary outreach program of on-the-spot training of missionaries and native church leaders in counseling techniques. Narramore also provides leadership for counseling training sessions in churches and other institutions throughout the country, as well as having a cassette ministry for home study. In 1970 the Narramore Institute founded the Rosemead Graduate School of Psychology, a state-accredited graduate institution, which also conducts an outpatient counseling service.

For all of these activities, staff are needed in this very specialized ministry. For further information write to the address in Rosemead. For information about careers in other institutions of this kind, consult the *Directory of Religious Organizations*, published by Consortium Press. This book lists some two hundred educational institutions on various levels and with several different specialties (see Appendix E).

BIBLE SOCIETIES

Another category of organizations that have the backing of local churches and denominations, but are independent in structure and support, are the Bible societies. Some of them are listed here.

The American Bible Society, 1865 Broadway, New York, NY 10023

The American Bible Society (ABS) dates back to 1816, when it was organized "to promote the distribution of the Holy Scriptures without doctrinal note or comment and without profit." The Society's program soon expanded from distribution in the U.S. to a worldwide outreach. The American Bible Society cooperates with the United Bible Societies, a worldwide organization, in a global coordination of Scripture translation, production, and distribution.

Through the labor of scholars and the efforts of translators, at least one book of the Bible has been translated and published by various Christian organizations in more than fifteen hundred languages and dialects.

To meet the needs for Scripture in current texts and formats, the ABS has recorded the Bible on tapes, records, and cassettes, and has provided the Scriptures in a wide variety of other formats and designs. With the use of color printing and paperback bindings, and the division of the Bible in "portions," distribution has soared, especially since the publication of the Bible in *Today's English Version*, widely known as "Good News for Modern Man." Its translation and publication were sponsored by the ABS.

For all of these activities the American Bible Society needs all kinds of personnel. Discounting those engaged in specialized activities such as translation and publication, which are sporadic, the ABS regularly employs some four hundred persons. For information about their needs, write to the New York headquarters or to one of the following regional addresses: 310 North Michigan Avenue, Chicago, IL 60601; 2220 Parklake Drive North, Atlanta, GA 30345; or 1460 Westwood Boulevard, Los Angeles, CA 90024.

United Bible Societies, P.O. Box 755, D-7, Stuttgart I, Germany

The United Bible Societies is the umbrella organization (the American Bible Society is a member) for independent national Bible societies that have as their purpose the widest possible distribution of the Holy Scriptures. Each of the national societies has its own staff, but in addition the United Bible Societies employs a group of full-time consultants in specialized fields: translation, linguistics, production, management, and distribution.

Bibles for the World, Box 805, Wheaton, IL 60187

Bibles for the World is a small, primarily direct-mail, operation. It has about thirty employees and occasional part-time help. Its purpose is the free distribution of the Bible throughout the world.

Laymen's National Bible Committee, Inc., 815 Second Avenue, New York, NY 10017

The Laymen's National Bible Committee is an organization with a very small paid staff, but a large group of volunteers whose purpose is "to promote Bible reading and study, the teaching of Bible materials in public education courses, church and synagogue attendance and religion in general." Founded in 1940, this organization's volunteers are primarily business people. The Bible Committee sponsors National Bible Week which, through various means, calls attention to the need for regular Bible reading. Founded by Protestants, this effort also has the support of Catholic and Jewish leadership.

Wycliffe Bible Translators, Inc.,
19891 Beach Boulevard, Huntington Beach, CA 92648

Since the Wycliffe Bible Translators is primarily concerned with work overseas, it is treated more fully in
chapter 5, International Career Opportunities, but is
mentioned here in connection with Bible work. Named
after John Wycliffe, the fourteenth-century translator of
the Bible into English, this organization was founded
forty years ago to meet the challenge of the many people who did not have the Bible available in their language. The organization's translation and teaching
programs currently involve work in more than six hundred languages. In addition to the address given here,
this active organization has five other regional offices
(see page 189).

Besides the organizations we have listed, the following should be investigated for career opportunities in
Bible-promoting organizations:

Bible Literature International
P.O. Box 477
Columbus, OH 43216

Gideon's International
2900 Lebanon Road
Nashville, TN 37214

New York International Bible Society
45 East 46th Street
New York, NY 10017

Pocket Testament League
117 Main Street
Lincoln Park, NJ 07035

World Home Bible League
16801 Van Dam Road
Holland, IL 60473

PUBLISHING

The various specialties (such as printer, writer, editor, and artist) involved in the field of publishing are covered in detail in chapter 2, in the section on publishing, but a great deal of the publishing of both periodicals and books is under the sponsorship of non–church-related companies. Any person interested in a career in religious publishing will want to examine in some detail the vast number of opportunities here. Both the production and the sale of Christian literature are largely in the hands of these independent organizations and companies.

Publishers

The Christian publishing industry is an expanding field and the need for skilled people continues to grow. Some of the typical positions in the industry are: artists, writers, editors (of books, curriculum, magazines, Bibles, and books about the Bible), advertising experts, sales persons (sales managers, trade representatives, telephone sales people), printers, purchasing agents, marketing experts, administrators, Christian education consultants, credit managers, accountants, secretaries, office workers, departmental managers, computer personnel, and the like.

A useful source of information about careers in publishing, especially with those companies that have an evangelical leaning, is the Evangelical Christian Publishers Association, P.O. Box 35, La Habra, CA 90631. Thirty-seven publishers are members. Many are also members of the Christian Booksellers Association (see below), but some of the smaller companies are not.

The following are some of the best-known of the publishers that specialize in religious books but are not connected officially with any denominational group. Anyone interested in a career in publishing should study the list of publications of these companies in order to determine which one would best fit his or her interests. To do so, write to the company, requesting a copy of its current catalog. Most of these companies specialize in book publishing, but some also publish periodicals. Questions about job openings should be directed to the personnel director.

Baker Book House
1019 Wealthy Street
Grand Rapids, MI 49506

Bethany Fellowship, Inc.
6820 Auto Club Road
Minneapolis MN 55438

Chosen Books
Lincoln, VA 22078

David C. Cook Publishing Co.
850 North Grove Avenue
Elgin, IL 60120

Creation House
Box 316
Carol Stream, IL 60187

Wm. B. Eerdmans
255 Jefferson Avenue SE,
Grand Rapids, MI 49502

Gospel Light Publications
P.O. Box 1591
Glendale, CA 91209

Inter-Varsity Press
P.O. Box 5
Downers Grove, IL 60515

Logos International
201 Church Street
Plainfield, NJ 07060

Moody Press
820 North LaSalle Street
Chicago, IL 60610

Morehouse-Barlow Co., Inc.
78 Danbury Road
Wilton, CT 06897

Thomas Nelson Inc.
407 Seventh Avenue South
Nashville, TN 37203

Fleming H. Revell Co.
Old Tappan, NJ 07675

Scripture Press Publications
1825 College Avenue
Wheaton IL, 60187

Sheed, Andrews, McMeel, Inc.
6700 Squibb Road,
Mission, KS 66202

Standard Publishing
8121 Hamilton Avenue
Cincinnati, OH 45231

Tyndale House
336 Gunderson Drive
Wheaton, IL 60187

Winston Press, Inc.
25 Groveland Terrace
Minneapolis, MN 55403

Word, Inc.
4800 Waco Drive
Waco, TX 76703

Zondervan Publishing House
1415 Lake Drive SE
Grand Rapids, MI 49506

In addition the following are general trade publishers that have strong religious offerings:

William B. Collins Publishing Company
2080 West 117th Street
Cleveland, OH 44111

Doubleday & Co.
245 Park Avenue
New York, NY 10017

Harper & Row
1700 Montgomery Street
San Francisco, CA 94111

Oxford University Press
200 Madison Avenue
New York, NY 10016

As we noted in chapter 2, Careers in Church-Wide Institutions and Offices, magazines and other periodicals offer an excellent opportunity for religious careers. This area of publishing is growing and rapidly changing. The best source for lists of religious magazines of an independent nature is in *Literary Market Place (LMP)*, an annual publication of the Bowker Company in New York. *LMP* can be found in most public libraries and in many bookstores. This book contains complete, up-to-date information about all magazines being published, as well as a categorized list that leads the reader to those magazines with a religious purpose and outlook. Another source of information about religious magazines is *The Writer's Market*, an annual publication of Writer's Digest Books, Cincinnati, OH. This, too, can be found in libraries and bookstores.

Booksellers

The sales end of the religious publishing business also provides many career opportunities. The Christian Bookseller's Association describes careers in bookselling as follows:

"The prospects for the future in Christian bookselling are very bright. The majority of Christian bookstores have shown good growth the past several years. In addition to the known trends, other factors are particularly encouraging.

"1. Marketing surveys indicate a return to the

smaller, specialized retail outlets, where customer service and individual attention is given. The Christian bookstore fits this pattern.

"2. We are living in a literary age—actually a 'communication revolution'—demanding more books, Bibles, and Christian educational materials every day.

"3. Publishers of Christian materials are meeting the challenge through research, development of materials, and marketing, thus giving the Christian Bookstore an added advantage.

"4. The Christian Booksellers Association has seen steady growth since 1950. In 1970 there were 950 CBA member bookstores with annual average gross sales of $46 thousand. By 1977 membership climbed to 2,350 with annual average gross sales of $94 thousand. Every indication is that the Christian bookselling industry is a growth industry."

These thousands of independent Christian bookstores involve the following typical positions: sales people (in the store, on the telephone, outside the store at conferences, etc.), audiovisual managers, stockroom and shipping-room personnel, office workers, bookkeepers, accountants, secretaries, Christian education consultants, mailroom managers, assistant managers, managers, departmental managers, purchasing agents, and so on.

The main source of information about independent Christian book publishing and selling nationwide is the Christian Booksellers Association. It is located at 2031 West Cheyenne Road, Colorado Springs, CO 80906. Both booksellers and publishers are members of this group. They publish a monthly trade magazine, *The Bookstore Journal.*

Writers

Persons interested in a career in religious journalism will find an abundance of opportunities for either full-time or part-time employment through denominational and interdenominational operations, as well as through the many independent Christian publishing agencies mentioned in this chapter. In addition, as has been noted, there is a need for writers of promotional and advertising material, and sometimes curriculum in independent organizations, such as those engaged primarily in evangelism. Writers are always needed, and the person interested in this kind of career should examine all avenues, not just the most obvious ones. The Christian Writer's Institute, Gunderson Drive and Schmale Road, Wheaton, IL 60187, is an organization that aids the writers of Christian literature. Through correspondence courses, as well as conferences and workshops, this organization enlists the aid of many successful writers and editors in the training of new writers of Christian material. Throughout the country there are annual writers conferences that serve the same purpose. Some of the better-known ones include the following:

Mount Hermon Christian Writers Conference
Box 413 W
Mount Hermon, CA 95041

Decision School of Christian Writing
Box 779
Minneapolis, MN 55440

Christian Writers Workshop
Forest Home, Inc.
Forest Falls, CA 92339

Brite Christian Writers Conference
11405 Farnam Circle
Omaha, NE 68154

Western North Carolina Christian Writers
Conference
Box 188
Black Mountain, NC 28711

St. David's Christian Writers Conference
Route 2
Cochranville, PA 19220

Christian Writers Conference
Warner Pacific College
2219 S.E. 68th Avenue
Portland, OR 97215

Other Employment Opportunities

Christian Literature Crusade, P.O. Box C, Fort Washington, PA 19034. The CLC is engaged primarily in overseas work, but we mention it here in connection with the publishing operations of non–church-related organizations. Founded in England in 1941, the CLC has grown to employ nearly five hundred persons who serve in forty countries and send the printed Christian message into more than sixty others. The CLC maintains book centers in strategic cities, which serve as bases of operation, sending out bookmobiles to distribute Christian literature. There is a constant need for personnel in the U.S. office of this growing organization. The CLC's own literature maintains that there are always one hundred immediate openings for workers in a variety of occupations related to publishing and evangelistic work.

Christian Life, Inc., Gundersen Drive and Schmale Road, Wheaton, IL 60287. Christian Life publishes and distributes several types of materials that are similar to those of other companies. We mentioned this company here because of two unusual publications that are important to the Christian bookselling trade. This company publishes *Christian Life,* a magazine distributed primarily through retail outlets selling religious books, records, films, and related products. In addition, the organization publishes *The Christian Bookseller,* a trade magazine for bookstore operators. A small operation with thirty-five employees, it is also a source of information about career opportunities in the whole book production and selling field.

UNILIT, 5600 N.E. Hassalo, Portland, OR 97213. A division of Tyndale Publishers, UNILIT is an unusual and rather new operation that has been important in the bookselling trade. Operating as a wholesale jobber, UNILIT provides the small bookstore with a buying service that makes it possible, especially for inexperienced bookstore operators, to get help in purchasing and stocking their stores. In addition to its buying services, UNILIT provides other help to store owners and managers, including a handbook entitled *Christian Bookstore Manual;* persons interested in this career will want to obtain a copy.

RADIO AND TELEVISION

One hardly knows where to begin to describe the burgeoning opportunities for careers in religious radio and television. National Religious Broadcasters (NRB), the main representative of the industry, reports an association of about nine hundred organizations that produce religious programs for radio and television or operate stations carrying predominantly religious programs. These groups that belong to the NRB are responsible for more than 70 percent of all religious radio and TV in the U.S., as well as for missionary broadcasting around the world. In the U.S. alone, NRB members reach an average weekly audience of more than 115 million by radio, and almost 14 million more by television.

Television

Because they are the most visible and employ the most people, let us examine the national religious television programs. These have multiplied in the last few years, making the local radio and television shows seem less significant. Perhaps the largest organization involved in religious television is the Christian Broadcasting Network (CBN) in Virginia Beach, Virginia. The main production of this network is the daily broadcast of the "700 Club," an evangelical version of the "Tonight Show." When it began, M. G. (Pat) Robertson, the moderator, asked seven hundred people each to give ten dollars a week to support this show—thus the name. This organization has blossomed into a huge conglomerate involving four television stations and six radio operations. It has an earth satellite that enables the show to be viewed anywhere in the world. CBN employs about eight hundred people, and has trained another nineteen thousand volunteer "counselors" to cover switchboards in every city in which the program is carried. CBN reports an annual budget of around $50 million!

A similar talk-show format is followed by the "PTL Club" (for Praise the Lord) broadcast out of Charlotte, North Carolina, with Jim Bakker at its head. This show, too, has boomed. As the fourth-largest purchaser of syndicated air time, with 198 affiliates, it employs some eight hundred people. From time to time this show has had financial problems, although at present it seems able to survive. Whether it does or not, it is ample demonstration of the fact that religious TV is big businessm

The "700 Club" reports annual offerings from listeners of $25 million. The August 12, 1978, *TV Guide* listed these other shows and their annual offerings as among the largest of the current TV religious programs: Church of God: $65 million; Billy Graham Evangelistic Association: $38 million; Thomas Road Baptist Church: $32.5 million; Garden Grove Community Church (Hour of Power): $10.9 million. None of these has the large staffs of the "700 Club," but they do offer career opportunities in religious television for hundreds of persons.

In addition to these programs, there are hundreds of smaller operations in the television field, offering new and interesting careers. The National Religious Broadcasters reports that its members are forming *one new Christian TV station per month*. The NRB distributes a brochure for those interested in setting up such a station. It is entitled "You Can Build and Operate a Christian TV Station," and is available from Quality Media Corporation, 4402 Bondale Drive, Columbia, GA 31907. In addition, these books and materials are available from the National Religious Broadcasters, Box 2254R,

Morristown, NJ 07960: *Annual Directory of Religious Broad-casting,* a comprehensive listing of all religious broadcasting in both radio and TV, and allied business services; *Religious Broadcasting Sourcebook,* a guide for those who want to know how to get started and succeed in religious radio and television; and *Religious Broadcasting,* a bimonthly magazine dealing with all aspects of religious broadcasting and the communications industry.

Radio

Radio, which has been in business much longer than television, is also becoming more and more involved with religious programming. The National Religious Broadcasters reports that its members are forming one new religious radio station *per week!* The February 4, 1979, *New York Times* confirmed this, quoting Philip Wallace, Director of Development for Christian Ministries Advertising, Inc., a company that buys time on radio and television stations for Christian organizations.

To prepare for careers in this seemingly limitless field, one needs all of the training and experience possible in the communications field. Colleges and universities are giving courses in communications, and many of them offer students the opportunity to gain actual experience by working on their own radio and TV stations, which are public broadcasting outlets.

In the specifically religious field there are some new materials and training sources becoming available, but the best guides of all come from the National Religious Broadcasters, as mentioned above. NRB describes its own services thus:

"Members benefit from a wide spectrum of staff services and cooperative efforts. Some key areas are:

—"Maintaining rapport with the broadcasting industry.
—"Cooperating with other media associations and keeping up to date on communications theory, technology and practice.
—"Fostering high professional standards through the implementation of the NRB code of ethics, the sponsorship of national and regional meetings which present opportunities for professional growth and development, and college-level training programs under the joint auspices of NRB and selected Christian colleges.
—"Gathering data on audiences, programs, communications effectiveness and worldwide broadcasting.
—"Cultivating spiritual depth through the messages of convention speakers, widening spiritual perspectives through the sharing of experiences and offering spiritual support through the ministry of prayer.
—"Providing liaison with legislative, regulatory and administrative government bodies. In addition to the NRB communication counsel in Washington, NRB regularly sends representatives to appear at Senate and House hearings and to take part in meetings with the executive branch of government."

CAMPS AND RETREATS

Many non–church-related organizations are involved in conducting camping programs or running retreat centers. These represent a variety of career possibilities. For detailed descriptions of the kind of people needed for such jobs, see chapter 2, Careers in Church-Wide Institutions and Offices.

Camps

Some of the largest and most effective camp programs are under the leadership of independent groups. Young Life (main office at P.O. Box 520, Colorado Springs, Co 80901), for example, is heavily involved in a camping program in its several locations. Much of its regular weekly activities with groups in high schools and communities is directed toward an eventual involvement in its camping activities. Other organizations discussed in this chapter, such as Campus Crusade for Christ and Youth for Christ, also have camping programs in which both permanent and seasonal staff are needed. One source of information on all kinds of camping programs, both church and non-church sponsored, is the American Camping Association (ACA), which can be reached by writing to Armin Ball, Executive Vice President, Bradford Woods, Martinsville, IN 46151. The ACA also has material available for the guidance of persons interested in the whole camping field.

For information about religious camps, one should write to Christian Camping International (CCI), P.O. Box 400, Somonauk, IL 60552. In April 1979, this organization listed more than 600 camps as members. A complete list of camps can be obtained by writing to the above address. CCI conducts international conventions of Christian camp managers and also has information about individual training and internship programs available in various locations. Anyone interested in a career in Christian camping will also want to read the new book, Werner Graendorf and Lloyd Mattson (eds), *An Introduction to Christian Camping* (Chicago: Moody Press, 1979).

Retreat Centers

As we stated also in chapter 2, in the section on camps and retreats, retreat centers exist in abundance in all parts of the United States. Many of these retreats are small and quite new; others are larger and have existed for a long time. Some have a large permanent staff of leaders and program persons; all of them need managers and food service and other support personnel. The following are some of the well-known retreat centers or agencies from which one might get further information.

Retreats International, 2999 West Spencer Street, Appleton, WI 54911. This is an organization that serves the lay retreat movement in the U.S. Catholic Church. It also directs the activities of several retreat houses in various parts of the country and issues a bimonthly newsletter, *Retreat World.*

Mount Hermon Christian Conference Center, Mount Hermon, CA 95041. This center, founded in 1906, is a non-profit, nondenominational evangelical arm of the church. A full-time staff of forty-five workers conducts its year-round program. This is supplemented by a summer staff of over two hundred. There are four separate camps under its management: the Conference Center, Ponderosa Lodge, Rewood Camp, and Sierra Treks (a back-packing satellite ministry).

Adult Christian Education Foundation, The Yahara Center,

159

Box 5305, Madison, WI 53705.   This foundation is the sponsor of the Bethel Series, a long range Christian education program used in some four thousand churches of all denominations in the U.S., Canada, and five foreign countries. The new Yahara Center is a conference facility that extends this ministry.

Geneva Point Center, Star Route 62, Box 469, Center Harbor, NY 03226.   This center is owned and operated by the Division of Christian Education of the National Council of Churches. For more than fifty years it has been of service as a retreat location for religious groups of all ages and denominational backgrounds.

Kirkridge, Bangor, PA 18013.   This is a rather new center offering several types of facilities for retreats, workshops, seminars, and other human renewal meetings. It has an active, year-round program, with most groups staying only three, but sometimes as long as eight, days.

Laity Lodge Foundation, P.O. Box 670, Kerrville, TX 78028.   This operation is part of a group of organizations concentrating on work with lay leadership in the churches—the sponsors of the National Conference on the Laity in Los Angeles in 1978.

Yokefellows International, 230 College Avenue, Richmond, IN 47374.   A largely volunteer organization with a limited staff, Yokefellows works as a catalytic agent in local churches. Each retreat center operating under the organization is autonomous and has a separate board of directors. Information about any of them can be obtained from the Yokefellows' address above.

Retreats are a growing phenomenon in the Christian world. They have been popular for many years in Catholic circles, and more recently have been set up by others as well. As the world becomes more and more pressured and hectic, the need for getting away from one's usual activities in order to find communion with God and oneself is bound to increase as well. The centers where such retreats are located are small in themselves, but together they represent a large area of career possibilities for the future.

SPECIALIZED SERVICE ORGANIZATIONS

In addition to the above categories, which cover only the most prominent of the hundreds of religious organizations at work in the United States, there are many non–church-related groups involved in services of a very specialized kind. The person interested in discovering religious careers in these should consult the *Directory of Organizations* available in the public library, as well as lists of groups in the publications of such organizations as the National Council of Churches or the National Association of Evangelicals. For purposes of example, however, we list here some of the specialized agencies that need employees with many different types of skills. These organizations are representative of hundreds of others in operation in the U.S. today.

Young Men's Christian Association, 291 Broadway, New York, NY 10007. The YMCA is just over one hundred years old. Organized to offer housing and Christian fellowship for young men, principally in cities, the YMCA soon developed the program of recreation and health for which it is well known. It also pioneered in camping and informal educational training, both of which it continues extensively today. There are 900 corporate YMCAs and a total of 1,800 individual member associations. It owns and operates 66 camps. Most of the career opportunities in the YMCA are as program directors, of which there are now about 6,000. Information about careers can be obtained from local YMCAs or the headquarters address given above.

Young Women's Christian Association, 600 Lexington Avenue, New York, NY 10022. Similar to the YMCA, the YWCA was originally established to care for the needs of young women in the cities by providing housing and Christian fellowship. Through the years the YWCA has also developed an extensive program of classes that appeal to both men and women of all ages. Its program is in need of personnel with various talents: center directors, youth and young adult specialists, executives, administrators, program coordinators, physical education instructors, and recreational directors; it also has a large staff of teachers for informal education classes of all kinds. Those interested in seeking a career in the YWCAs should send requests to the Membership-Leadership Development of the National Board at the address listed above.

Christian Children's Fund, P.O. Box 26511, Richmond, VA 23261. The Christian Children's Fund (CCF) is representative of many other organizations that are not in themselves religious, but have a religious orientation and are staffed by persons with a religious commitment. The CCF grew out of the early efforts in 1938 of its founder, Dr. Verent Mills, to minister to the needs of Chinese children who were refugees as a result of the Japanese invasion of China. The CCF has continued to feed and give aid to suffering children, and is now at work in six locations around the world with a family help program, day care centers, and other programs that minister to the homeless, the hungry, and the handicapped. It is supported by a large group of sponsors. The personnel of the CCF administers the program through its various centers.

Christian Theatre Artists Guild, 1 Groveland Terrace, P.O. Box 14157, Minneapolis, MN 55414. The Christian Theatre Artists Guild organization does not employ many persons; rather, it serves as a clearing house for the religious theatre that is produced around the country. It compiles an annual directory of theatre troupes and art organizations "designed to honor God and serve Jesus Christ." Its members fall into two categories: organizations (usually theatre groups), of which the Guild lists some 130, and individuals (usually directors), of which there are 50. Persons interested in a career in the theatre related to Christian commitment should contact the Guild at the above address.

The John Milton Society for the Blind, 29 West 34th Street, New York, NY 10001. The John Milton Society for the Blind is a Christian ministry utilizing religious literature, which it prints for the use of the blind and the visually impaired. The society publishes Christian materials in braille, large type, and on talking-book records. It also publishes a monthly magazine, a monthly religious digest for young readers, and a Sunday-school quarterly. Its personnel needs are small, but the organization is like many others with religious foundations that minister to disadvantaged handicapped persons.

Religion in American Life, 815 Second Avenue, New York, NY 10017. Religion in American Life is a cooperative program involving some forty national religious groups from all major faiths working together to encourage attendance at worship and participation in religious programs. It plans and conducts an annual advertising campaign utilizing all types of media, and helps organize community programs, which provide local application of its national message.

5

International Career Opportunities

From its very earliest days, Christianity has had a world-wide thrust. After the day of Pentecost reported in the Book of Acts in the New Testament, the disciples of Jesus became "apostles," sent out by him "to make disciples of all nations" to the "uttermost parts of the earth." Immediately upon his conversion to Christianity, Saul of Tarsus changed his name to Paul, in line with his new-found faith, and took off on his journeys around the then-known world surrounding the Mediterranean in order to tell others of what had happened to him.

One could follow this pattern through the history of the church—the Christianizing of Europe, the planting of the church in the New World after the arrival of Columbus, the great missionary movements of the nineteenth century, the missionary orders of the Catholic Church, and all the way down to the many new and different overseas ministries of Christians today.

Anyone thinking about a career in religion will also

164

want to consider international opportunities, which are abundant and more diverse today then ever before. In fact, one hardly knows where to begin to survey the situation. Just as everything in the world moves at such a rapid pace, the picture in world missions is also changing rapidly.

One ought logically to begin to look at opportunities in one's own church or denomination. Every church body has a board or group charged with the responsibility of seeking candidates, training them, and supporting them in mission endeavors around the world. Beyond this there are nondenominational or independent groups that support overseas work of various kinds. Some of these are large and well established. Many of them are small and new. In addition, there are those movements and specialized ministries that recruit personnel to do specific work—medical missions, relief work, education, translation and distribution of the Scriptures, radio and television, Gospel recordings and cassettes. There is even a missionary aviation service for reaching remote parts of the world.

We will look at all of these in this chapter, but first let us get some idea of what the missionary endeavor is like today. In the nineteenth and early twentieth centuries, missionary work could be quite simply described, and the type of activity in which the missionary engaged was always the same. Those who went to serve in foreign fields were almost always ordained clergy who saw their calling as evangelistic: to preach the Gospel, convert the natives, and establish churches wherever possible. Along with the preaching evangelists, there were sometimes teachers (often missionaries' wives) who started schools, or nurses and doctors who established clinics and eventually hospitals.

But this picture has radically changed for a number of reasons. The churches established by those early missionaries grew and became strong. Along with the independence of many former colonial nations has come the movement toward independence for the native churches. The missionary is no longer the father figure—the great white God; he or she is the coworker and helper under the supervision of native church leadership. Sometimes political changes have meant the complete removal of the traditional foreign missionary, who was considered by some to be a "colonialist." Today the only kind of work possible in some areas is of a completely different nature from that of the past.

Thus both the recruiting and training of overseas workers has changed considerably. The number of occupational skills needed has expanded, and the need for unordained personnel multiplied. One could look at the long list supplied by Intercristo, the Christian employment agency in Seattle (discussed in detail in chapter 4, Careers in Non Church-Related Organizations), and duplicate this for work on the international level. But to be more specific about international needs, let us look at the following list compiled by the Inter-Varsity Christian Fellowship and distributed by Overseas Crusades.

TYPES OF MISSIONARY PERSONNEL NEEDED

Evangelism and Church Development

Evangelists, general workers, pioneer workers, children's workers, orphanage personnel, youth workers, women's workers, student workers, servicemen's centers.

Business and Administration

Accountants, bookkeepers, business managers, general office workers, secretaries and/or stenographers, typists, treasurer, buyer and export manager, mission home management, hostess for headquarters and guest home.

Education

Principals or supervisors, elementary teachers, secondary teachers, Bible-school teachers, college/university teachers, vocational or industrial teachers, seminary teachers, teachers for missionary children, houseparents for missionary children.

Literature

Artists, bookstore managers, editors, photographers, printers, writers, distribution managers, advertising managers.

Linguistic Work and Translation

Linguists and/or translators, literacy campaigns.

Medicine and Dentistry

Doctors, hospital administrators, nurses, nursing instructors, medical-school instructors, technicians and/or technologists, pharmacists, therapists, dentists, dental assistants and technicians, optometrists, dieticians.

Radio and Recording

Announcers, continuity writers, musicians, office personnel, program directors, producers, technicians and engineers, TV personnel.

Industrial Skills

Agriculturists, builders, mechanics, airplane pilots and pilot-mechanics, maintenance men.

The following information about overseas missions today is based on material given in the 1976 edition of the *Mission Handbook*,[1] published by the Mission Advanced Research and Communication Center (MARC). This organization queried 750 churches and agencies that have overseas personnel; 620 of them responded. The following material is based on that information.

WHO ARE THE OVERSEAS PERSONNEL?

Protestant Missionaries

There was a time in the history of the missionary movement when it was understood that a missionary was someone who was making a lifetime career of serving another people, usually outside the borders of his or her own country. Such a definition is no longer accu-

[1] Taken from the 11th edition of the *Mission Handbook*, published by Missions Advanced Research and Communication Center (MARC), a ministry of World Vision International, 919 W. Huntington Drive, Monrovia, CA 91016. Used by permission.

rate; today many missionaries plan in advance to interrupt or discontinue this career at some point. The concept of a missionary career is thus taking its place alongside other career concepts such as engineering, medicine, or law. It is a phenomenon of present North American society that individuals move in and out of such careers with a surprising degree of ease. Many men and women embarking upon a career in overseas ministry fully expect that at some point in their life they will change careers or return to their home country.

The total overseas community includes a growing number of "short-term" personnel. This expression defies definition: Some people serve for less than a week, while thousands of others serve for periods ranging from one to six years, or serve more than one short term. Most, but not all agencies involved with overseas missionaries include short-term personnel in their totals. In order to establish a consistent base line we have assumed that *all* short-termers listed in MARC's *Mission Handbook* should be included in the grand total of Protestant North Americans who served any time overseas during 1975. Where the short-term program was less than twelve months, totals have been factored and an equivalent full-time total derived to describe how many individuals may be serving as "overseas personnel" at any one time during the year.

Overseas Staff. It is estimated that about 50,000 to 55,000 Protestants, of which 65 to 70 percent come from North America (the U.S. and Canada), work in 182 foreign countries. About forty-four percent are men, and fifty-six percent, women. The U.S. mission force has continued to increase since 1969, whereas church membership reversed a declining trend only in 1974.

The Canadian missions force as a percentage of church membership has increased steadily since 1965. From another perspective, the total number of overseas personnel has kept up approximately with the percentage of population increase in the U.S.

Short-Term Protestant Personnel. Some of those serving overseas are full-time "career" personnel; others go abroad for a limited term. It should be noted that, since 1970, more and more of the overseas force has been made up of short-term personnel. In 1975, they comprised about 16 percent of the total work force abroad. This essentially means that career personnel are being replaced by limited-term personnel.

New Personnel. Of the agencies responding to MARC's questionnaire, 295 reported a total of 4,476 new personnel for the two-year period 1974/1975 (6 percent of the total force). This is about the same percentage that had been reported in previous years.

Non–North-American Personnel. MARC's questionnaire sought to determine the number of non-North Americans serving with each agency as overseas personnel; i.e., serving outside their home country. This question was intended to help determine the extent of internationalization of the predominantly North American missionary force. These persons are distinct from what are often termed "nationals," citizens of another country who are associated with a foreign mission in some capacity but who remain in their home country, and whose numbers run into the tens of thousands.

Two hundred fifty-six agencies reported over four thousand non–North-American personnel serving in other countries, compared with the 3,649 of them working in other countries reported by 107 agencies in 1972.

Other Religious Missionary Movements

Although the MARC *Handbook* primarily describes the missionary activity of Protestant agencies, readers should be aware of other religious missionary movements emanating from North America. Four major non-Protestant bodies are covered here: Roman Catholic, Orthodox, Latter-Day Saints (Mormon), and Jehovah's Witnesses.

Roman Catholic. In 1968, the number of U.S. Catholic missionaries serving outside the forty-eight contiguous states numbered nearly ten thousand. Since then, however, this number has declined steadily to approximately seven thousand in 1975. These missionaries are active in Alaska, Hawaii, and Canada, as well as abroad, with most serving in the Philippines, Japan, Puerto Rico, and Latin America. They also work in Asia, Africa, Oceania, with a handful in other parts of North America and in Europe. Unlike the world Protestant missionary force, less than 25 percent of the Catholic missionary personnel comes from this continent.

Orthodox Churches. Of the three traditional branches of Christianity, the Orthodox Church is the smallest but, in some senses, the oldest. The Orthodox churches are subdivided into three major groupings: Eastern (Chalcedonian), Oriental (non-Chalcedonian), and Assyrian (Nestorian). Orthodoxy is composed of self-governing and mutually independent national churches throughout the world. There are more than a dozen such church bodies in North America, with a total constituency of approximately 4.1 million people, most of whom live in the United States. The Orthodox churches in North America are essentially self-governing, and with each

171

one responsible for the missionary activity within its territory. Although very few missionaries are sent from North America to other countries, the formation of missions departments at church headquarters and the teaching of mission courses in the seminaries and theological schools suggests a growing interest in this aspect of ministry.

Latter-Day Saints (Mormons).   Of the four bodies of Latter-Day Saints listed in the *1976 Yearbook of American and Canadian Churches*, the Church of Jesus Christ of Latter-Day Saints is the largest. Since it is common for each Mormon man to serve a two-year church term before moving on to a secular career, many of them serve short terms as missionaries, either in North America or overseas. The result is that there are approximately twenty thousand Mormon missionaries serving in approximately sixty different countries.

Jehovah's Witnesses. The Jehovah's Witnesses are known for their extensive activity in visitation and literature distribution. As all members are considered ministers, the number of persons actually being sent abroad as missionaries is relatively small.

Short-Termer Defined

What is a "short-termer"? Some years ago the question could have been answered easily: a missionary who was not planning to make overseas ministries his or her career. However, in recent years this definition has changed as the concept of a missionary career changes dramatically. At one time almost all missionaries thought of their calling as for a lifetime. Others take up a missionary career for eight or ten years in mid-life. More and more North American young people are spending a few days to two months in some form of overseas experience. Some mission agencies have recognized this trend and are commissioning missionaries for only one term of service at a time.

Continuing Overseas Careers

"Does a short-term career often lead to a more permanent career in overseas ministry? What percentage of short-termers returns to a career in your agency? To the best of your knowledge, what percentage of the short-termers you have goes into any later overseas career service?" The last question was answered by numbers ranging from 0 to 99 percent, with the average at about 25 percent. Of the 640 short-termers represented by the agencies, 147 of these, or 23 percent, reportedly returned to service in their original agency.

MISSIONARY AGENCIES

Between the 1880s and 1945, missionary agencies were founded at the rate of thirty to forty per decade. The real impetus to establish Protestant missionary organizations from North America came after World War II (over 100 were formed during the 1950s), although the rate has slowed somewhat. The increasing complexity of the modern world has encouraged specialization among organizations, and these include mission agencies. The demands of broadcasting, literature production, language analysis, and transportation (to name only a few) have brought into being agencies that have a specialized ministry in such areas.

THE DECISION TO BECOME A MISSIONARY

Once a decision is made to actively seek employment as an overseas religious worker, what is the first step? Intercristo's *Directory of Christian Work Opportunities* recommends that the prospective missionary ask himself or herself the following questions before pursuing the matter further.

• Why do I want to go overseas—what's my real motivation? Is my motivation just adventure, something "different," or to see the world? Or do I really want to serve and learn?

• What are my objectives? Are my goals realistic on what I can achieve or do I hope to "change the world"? Can I set one or two specific things I would like to see happen—in my service to others or in my own growth?

• What are my expectations about missionaries? Do I view them as "super-people" or, more realistically, as someone like myself (with all my human frailties), who have responded and done what they think God has called them to do?

• What is my view of myself as an American? Do I recognize my own limited cultural views of power, economic values, and governmental/political structures? Do I recognize the value of other cultures, or is "different" the same as "inferior"?

• What do I understand about the biblical principles of suffering, sacrifice, and faithfulness?

• What is my attitude about those nationals I want to work with? Am I superior in my attitude or do I go with a spirit of a servant? Do I demonstrate that kind of spirit here?

• What experience have I had with other ethnic groups here and how did I get along? Have I been threatened by those experiences?

• Do I have a flexible, adaptive spirit? Can I "roll with the punches" or do things have to be highly structured for me?

• How do I do in "strange" or new circumstances? Do I find those situations challenging, something to be anticipated—or are those situations threatening to me?

• What do I know about the Scripture's outline of God's plan for the church and where "missionaries" or cross-cultural Christian service fits in? [2]

The kind of people needed for overseas service in religious occupations is also rather well summed up in the literature of the Evangelical Alliance Mission, which states it this way:

The missionary candidate should be:
   Self-reliant but not self-sufficient
   Energetic but not self-seeking
   Steadfast but not stubborn
   Tactful but not timid
   Serious but not sullen
   Loyal but not sectarian
   Immovable but not stationary
   Gentle but not hypersensitive

[2] From *Directory of Christian Work Opportunities.* © 1978 The International Christian Organization. Used by permission.

Tender-hearted but not touchy
Conscientious but not a perfectionist
Disciplined but not demanding
Generous but not gullible
Meek but not weak
Humorous but not hilarious
Friendly but not familiar
Holy but not holier-than-thou
Discerning but not critical
Progressive but not pretentious

AGENCIES SPONSORING OVERSEAS EMPLOYMENT

Churches

The churches are by far the largest employers of overseas religious personnel. As reported by the Mission Advanced Research and Convention Center, the largest sponsors of missionaries are the denominations or faith groups. Anyone looking for an opportunity for service overseas ought to first investigate his or her own church's offerings. Of the forty-five thousand persons serving in overseas religious posts reported by MARC, perhaps twenty-five thousand of these are serving under the sponsorship of one of the denominations or faith groups.

Persons interested in finding out about what kinds of missionary positions are available in his or her own denomination should write to its board of world missions at its headquarters or world mission office. The following are the world mission addresses for some of the major denominations in the U.S.

Assemblies of God: Director of Foreign Missions, 1445 Booneville Avenue, Springfield, MO, 65802

American Baptists: World Mission Support, American Baptist Churches, Valley Forge, PA 19481

Southern Baptists: Foreign Mission Board, Southern Baptist Convention, 3806 Monument Avenue, Richmond, VA 23230

Christian Church (Disciples): Division of Overseas Ministries, 222 South Downey Avenue, Box 1986, Indianapolis, IN 46206

Episcopal Church: Executive for Mission, 815 Second Avenue, New York, NY 10017

American Lutheran Church: Board for World Mission, 422 South Fifth Street, Minneapolis, MN 55415

Lutheran Church in America: Division for World Mission, 231 Madison Avenue, New York, NY 10016

Lutheran Church-Missouri Synod: Board for Missions, 500 North Broadway, St. Louis, MO 63102

Methodists: United Methodist Church, Board of Global Ministries, 475 Riverside Drive, New York, NY 10027

Mormons: Church of Jesus Christ of Latter Day Saints, 47 East South Temple Street, Salt Lake City, UT 84111

Greek Orthodox Archdiocese of North and South America: 8–10 East 79th Street, New York, NY 10021

Russian Orthodox Church in America: P.O. Box 675, Syosset, NY 11701

Presbyterian Church in the U.S.: Division of International Missions, 341 Ponce de Leon Avenue N.E., Atlanta, GA 30308

United Presbyterian Church, U.S.A.: Program Agency, 475 Riverside Drive, New York, NY 10027

Roman Catholic Church: United States Catholic Conference, 1312 Massachusetts Avenue N.W., Washington, DC 20005

United Church of Christ: Board of World Ministries, 475 Riverside Drive, New York, NY 10027

Information on world missions operations of smaller denominations and world faith groups can be obtained from the directory of churches in the *Yearbook of American and Canadian Churches* (Abingdon Press).

All of these boards publish materials that are helpful to the missionary candidate in knowing what is expected in the field, what kinds of positions are available, what training is provided, and what the candidate should do to find a suitable position. Since overseas service is more complicated than the usual church employment (including the fact that one must have some knowledge of a foreign language and an understanding of another culture, as well as an awareness that one will feel uprooted), more guidance is given to foreign service personnel than to those in other church occupations.

From time to time denominations make up lists of openings that they share with other denominations. The Division of Overseas Ministries of the National Council of Churches, 475 Riverside Drive, New York, NY 10027, acts as a clearing house for materials from all denominations—both those that belong to the Council and those that do not.

In addition to their denominational headquarters and boards of world missions, many of the churches work through their national faith group agencies in the placement of personnel overseas, particularly in the case of relief work or other social-service-oriented positions, which are usually cooperative, involving the faith group on a world-wide basis. Agencies that place overseas personnel are the Lutheran World Federation, which maintains a U.S. office at 360 Park Avenue South, New York, NY 10010; The Mennonite Central Committee, located at 21 South 12th Street, Akron, PA 17501; and the Association of Baptists for World Evangelism, 1720 Springdale Road, Cherry Hill, NJ 08034. Some denominational groups also serve as clearing houses for specialized services. One such organization is the Catholic Medical Mission Board (10 West 17th Street, New York, NY 10011), which recruits and assigns medical and paramedical personnel as well as carries out other services for its medical mission installations. However, none of the foregoing agencies takes the place of the main missionary recruitment work of the individual denominations.

A great number of the Roman Catholic missionaries serving throughout the world are sent by the various orders of the church rather than through the U.S. Catholic Conference. Therefore, someone interested in service in this church ought to examine the lists of Catholic orders and their programs. Perhaps the most up-to-date analyses of overseas work by Catholic groups are in the two books from Paulist Press: *Ministries for the Lord, A Resource Guide and Directory of Church Vocations for Men* and *Images of Women in Mission, A Resource Guide and Directory of Church Vocations for Women.*

Anyone studying overseas opportunities for Christian service ought also to look into the possibility of involvement in a volunteer overseas program as a means of getting acquainted with the field. Every denomination now has a volunteer program; and some are very extensive. Volunteers are usually sent to a foreign field for a briefer time than the regularly employed full-time missionary, and generally are expected to serve without receiving a salary, although most of the time travel expenses and room and board are taken care of during the period of service. For more information inquire at your denomination's world mission board (or volunteer service board, if it has one) or write to the Division of Overseas Ministries of the National Council of Churches, 475 Riverside Drive, New York, NY 10027. The Council acts as a clearing house for volunteers as well as others. A further discussion of volunteer work of all kinds is found in chapter 6, Part-Time, Seasonal, and Independent Careers. One can also get much information about overseas volunteer opportunities from any of the following organizations:

International Liaison, U.S. Catholic Coordinating Center for Lay Volunteer Mission
1234 Massachusetts Avenue NW
Washington, DC 20005

Christian Service Corps
1509 Sixteenth Street NW
Washington, DC 20036

Commission on Voluntary Service and Action
c/o J. Wilbur Patterson
United Presbyterian Church
475 Riverside Drive
New York, NY 10027

Independent Agencies

In the last two decades some of the largest employers of religious personnel in overseas work have been the independent agencies that have come into being in the last thirty years. We have already discussed some of these agencies in chapter 4, Careers in Non–Church-Related Organizations. For many of them, international work is their largest career area.

For example, in the listing of some twenty thousand openings for workers in the more than six hundred religious agencies listed in the *1979 Directory of Christian Work Opportunities* published by Intercristo, fully three-fourths of the jobs listed are overseas. Therefore, anyone interested in this kind of religious career cannot afford to pass up the opportunity of examining carefully what is being offered by these groups.

As reported in the MARC statistics mentioned previously, the vast majority of these new groups are small, but some, like World Vision International, are among the top ten agencies (including the churches) in terms of annual budgets. At least twenty-five thousand persons are employed overseas by independent religious agencies. With the preponderance of short-term (six months to three years) possibilities in this group, there is both a constant turnover and a continuing need for personnel.

Intergroup Agencies

Let us begin by examining the services of agencies that work with several independent mission organizations. We have already mentioned above the services of MARC, located at 919 West Huntington Drive, Monrovia, CA 91016. In addition to its triennial publication of the *Mission Handbook*, MARC can be very helpful in supplying other information needed by overseas mission candidates. Intercristo (P.O. Box 9329, Seattle, WA 98109) publishes the annual *Directory of Christian Work Opportunities*. It also provides other services to both employing agencies and persons looking for careers. Intercristo has counseling services on both an individual and a group basis for persons seeking help in determining their future in religious employment. It also offers career guidance for high school and college underclassmen.

There are at least two major agencies set up as clearing houses for the independent groups. The Interdenominational Foreign Mission Association, at P.O. Box 392, Wheaton, IL 69187, is one of these. The Association's name is a bit misleading since it is a fellowship of foreign mission societies *without* denominational affiliation, and was established for this purpose in 1917. Forty-eight missions are members of this group, which also acts as a clearing house for mission information for these groups and publishes frequent lists of world-wide opportunities and current needs of its members. The Association uses the services of such organizations as Intercristo and MARC in order to recruit personnel. It also publishes helpful materials for mission candidates. A somewhat similar group, and one that cooperates with the Association and offers another source of information about mission opportunities among evangelical societies, is Evangelical Mission Information Service, Box 794, Wheaton, IL 60187. This is a service organization for the Evangelical Foreign Missions Association and the Interdenominational Foreign Mission Association.

We will not attempt to list all of the independent agencies that are using overseas missionary personnel and thus represent international career possibilities. These are available from other sources, as listed above. However, the following is a sampling of eight typical agencies that use a fairly large number of personnel. A look at what they offer and some of the opportunities

through their services will give the reader an understanding of what is available through the other five
hundred or more agencies.

*Africa Inland Mission, Crooked Hill Road, Pearl River, NY
10965.* This nondenominational organization supports
some nine hundred missionaries. It sends workers into
East and Central Africa, the islands of the Indian Ocean,
and urban centers in the United States. Its objectives are
to recruit and train all types of mission personnel, plant
churches that will outlast the missionary presence, assist
national churches in their development, and create a
growing missionary spirit among home constituencies.
Medical missions is one of AIM's specialities; it maintains twelve hospitals in the fields.

*Agape Movement, Campus Crusade for Christ, Arrowhead
Springs, San Bernardino, CA 92414.* This is a new and
fast growing section of the Campus Crusade ministry.
The movement describes its purpose thus: "To recruit,
train, and send into other nations laymen able to share
their faith, disciple believers, aid national believers in
the implementation of their strategies for reaching their
people for Christ and contribute to the physical and
social needs of other people through the practice of
vocational and professional skills." The goal of this
movement is to train and send to other countries one
hundred thousand laymen by the end of 1980. In addition, the leaders plan to train nationals from every
country in the world in the cause of Christ, to use
professional and vocational knowledge and skills to
make significant contributions to international communities in demonstration of the love of Christ, and to aid
existing evangelical organizations and churches around
the world in taking the Gospel to every person in the
world. The Agape Movement includes a whole gamut

of occupations described in chapter 4, Careers in Non–Church-Related Organizations. In 1978, the Agape Movement leaders said they needed 500 persons immediately, and they anticipated that this need would expand. Training centers for Agape workers are being established in many areas. In the 1979 *Directory of Christian Work Opportunities*, the Agape Movement devoted seven and a half pages to listing its openings at the time of publication!

Christians in Action, Admissions Coordinator, Box 7271, 350 East Market Street, Long Beach, CA 90807. This is primarily a church-planting missionary organization. It has some one hundred twenty international workers, missionaries, and appointed candidates serving on five continents. Training schools operate in several locations in addition to the one at its headquarters. Classroom instruction is coupled with supervised field experience in personal evangelism. The primary thrust of Christians in Action is to train lay persons as individual missionaries. It also conducts a radio and TV ministry.

Great Europe Mission, P.O. Box 668, Wheaton, IL 60187. This organization is a bit different from most groups who are sending personnel overseas. Its purpose is to develop evangelical churches in Europe and provide theological training for clergy and lay leaders. Since its objective is to train leadership, most of the two hundred overseas jobs of this organization are for teachers in Bible Institutes and seminaries. Although most of these posts are filled by ordained personnel, there are other positions available to the unordained such as those for secretaries, business and public relations personnel, and some teaching positions not requiring theological training. This small organization is representative of many independent groups set up to minister to a special need in one area of the world.

Overseas Crusades, P.O. Box 66, Santa Clara, CA 95052. The objective of this organization is to reach a total of one thousand missionaries in fifteen years. Its stated purpose is "to work cross culturally with Christian believers and their church leadership in reaching the nations as a united missionary team." The organization uses various methods to reach its goal: publications, conferences, distribution of literature, classes in Bible reading and study, and assisting established missions with special vocational skills. The various skills requested by Overseas Crusades were used above as representative of all mission endeavors.

The Evangelical Alliance Mission, P.O. Box 969, Wheaton, IL 60187. TEAM has been planting churches for more than eighty-five years, first in northwest China and now throughout the world. More than one thousand active missionaries are evangelizing unreached areas and helping new Christians and young churches with their programs. TEAM is a faith mission without denominational affiliation, and has headquarters in Canada and Australia as well as the United States. It has a varied program of full-time service, in addition to an associate program for short-term missionaries and a summer program. In 1979 there were about four hundred openings in Africa, Asia, Latin America, and some European countries.

United World Mission, Box 8000, St. Petersburg, FL 33738. This is basically a church planning and developing agency ministering in seventeen countries on four continents. In addition to its church-related activities, this mission has worked closely with the special needs of the countries in which it finds itself, such as in the reconstruction of homes and churches in Guatemala, building an eye clinic in Mali, digging wells and so on. Priority in all missions is given to teaching workers in each country to lead their own churches and train their own people.

World Vision International, Personnel Director, 919 West Huntington Drive, Monrovia, CA 91016. This large independent operation was founded primarily to do refugee work among children, but has expanded its overseas ministry to include many other activities as well. Besides caring for many children abroad, it provides emergency relief, supports medium-range development programs to help people become self-sufficient, provides Christian leadership training, supports direct evangelistic activities and programs of national churches or mission groups, and challenges English-speaking people to respond to the needs of the suffering throughout the world. This vast program has about four hundred employees in the United States and about two thousand overseas. In addition to the *Handbook of Missions* mentioned previously, World Vision publishes a monthly magazine, a monthly newsletter for Christian leaders, and a quarterly dealing with world needs.

Specialized Agencies

Some religious agencies have been set up to provide very specialized services for international workers. There are many of these, but we will look at six that offer some particularly interesting and challenging career opportunities.

Bible Translators on Tape, Box 2500, Cedar Hill, TX 75104. Bible Translators on Tape (BTT) gained its inspiration from the late Dr. Frank Laubach, the great campaigner against world illiteracy. In his book, *The Silent Billion*, Laubach wrote about the one billion people over the age of fifteen who cannot read. These are "the most bruised people on this planet," he said, "naked, hungry, fallen among thieves, sick, imprisoned in mind and soul, afraid of educated men in this world and of demons in the next." In addition, illiteracy is rapidly increasing because the population in many illiterate areas is exploding. Bible Translators on Tape makes cassette tapes of portions of the Bible and other messages in many languages and provides these to remote regions along with "Crankasettes," spring-powered tape players. BTT needs translators as well as recording technologists and distributors; the latter are responsible for training people abroad in the use of the cassettes. This new, unusual, and expanding mission reports a constant need for new personnel, with many more openings than it is able to fill.

Christian Literature Crusade, Fort Washington, PA 19034. Founded in England in 1941, the CLC maintains offices in London, Australia, and New Zealand. Its basic purpose is the dissemination of Christian literature, primarily through book centers, which have been established throughout the world. Bookmobiles and deputation teams sell and distribute this literature wherever there is a need. More than four hundred persons are employed by CLC in its publication and distribution program. It is in constant need of book-center missionaries, bookmobile personnel, office workers, secretaries, accountants, and other business personnel, as well as journalists, editors, translators, artists, and printers.

Far East Broadcasting Company, P.O. Box 1, La Mirada, CA

187

90638. This group describes itself as "an extra-de-nominational radio missionary enterprise." In coopera-tion with existing missionary efforts, it runs Gospel broadcasting stations, provides all kinds of electronic equipment, and assists others engaged in this form of Christian work. It concentrates on broadcasting the Gospel to the Orient and South America, with an em-phasis on Communist countries. FEB currently employs more than six hundred people, and is actively seeking new personnel: engineers, programmers, script writers, and other office and technical workers, for its program of broadcasting the Gospel. It publishes a monthly mag-azine as well as other literature to explain its work.

Gospel Recordings International, 122 Glendale Boulevard, Los Angeles, CA 90026. In some respects this organization resembles the Bible Translators on Tape. Its purpose is to "reach the unevangelized tribes of the world in their own heart language." It is a world-wide evangelical mis-sionary organization designed to assist recognized evan-gelical groups or individuals by manufacturing and providing foreign-language records, cassette tapes, and equipment to play these in order to do evangelic work and teach basic Christian ideas to the illiterate. Besides the obvious need for production personnel, this group is seeking persons skilled in business management, writ-ing, mail order, photography, printing, and the like. Along with a need for full-time workers, Gospel Re-cordings has a three-month interim colaborer program, a volunteer activity open especially to young people interested in a mission experience of a special kind.

Missionary Aviation Fellowship, Box 2828, Fullerton, CA 92633. This unique organization provides air support for Christian churches around the world by flying hundreds of missionaries to areas of the world that would otherwise be inaccessible. The main need in this organization is for qualified pilots for the more than fifty aircraft that are flown to Africa, Asia, and Latin America. Pilots are expected to be familiar with and sympathetic toward the Christian missionary program. In addition to pilots, mechanics, radio technicians, accoun̄ tants, administrators, builders, researchers, educators, and support staff are needed.

Wycliffe Bible Translators, Inc., 19891 Beach Boulevard, Huntington Beach, CA 92648. This large and effective organization was founded to "forward the task of propagating the Gospel by putting the Word of God into all the tribal tongues of earth in which it does not yet exist." Wycliffe is meeting this challenge by sending hundreds of young people to remote areas of the world to live among and learn the languages of these people. The missionaries then translate the Bible into the languages. More than five hundred languages are currently being studied, and portions of the Scripture have been translated into over three hundred others. Wycliffe is an international organization using the services of translators from many countries working in hundreds of minority languages. The positions of linguists, translators, and literacy specialists are filled only by career workers, but the many other posts are filled by either career workers or short-term assistants. More information about career opportunities can be obtained from the address given above or from one of the following regional offices:

524 NE 118th Avenue
Portland, OR 97220

1 South 210 Summit Avenue
Oakbrook Terrace
Villa Park, IL 60181

5385 Five Forks Road
Stone Mountain, GA 30087

6231 Leesburg Pike
Falls Church, VA 22044

730 Mercury Avenue
Duncanville, TX 75137

PREPARATION AND TRAINING FOR OVERSEAS EMPLOYMENT

In many ways the preparation for a career in international religious work is different from that for other careers in religion. One must almost always know at least one other language, and sometimes several of its dialects as well. Adaptability to new situations and conditions is a good quality for anyone in a religious occupation, but for an overseas worker with intercultural adjustments to be made, it is essential. Because the foreign worker is away from old friends and familiar surroundings, there is a greater need than usual for cooperative teamwork among the mission's staff. In many places the work requires that the staff be together around the clock. The overseas worker must also be self-reliant under new circumstances and in unusual ways. There is not as much work supervision as one is used to, nor is there as much chance to compare one's job with persons in similar situations. The missionary's existence is often a lonely one, and distances from home and family are great. All of these conditions must be

taken into consideration by the candidate for an overseas post.

Mission boards and agencies are quite aware of these
considerations, and consequently devote more time and
attention to preparing workers for these positions than
for work in the homeland. Many missions have orientation programs for their workers and offer continuing
education opportunities during vacations and furloughs.
Some boards have a missionary internship program
where prospective employees serve a period of some
months under the supervision of a more experienced
missionary while they adjust to people of another land
and culture.

Information about some of these specialized training
programs is available from the Division of Overseas
Ministries of the National Council of Churches, 475
Riverside Drive, New York, NY 10027, or the United
States Catholic Missions Council, 1302 18th Street NW,
Washington, DC 20036. In addition, one can write directly to some of the training centers, of which nineteen
were listed in a 1978–79 brochure published jointly by
the two above groups. We list some of those that are
especially equipped to train missionaries and prospective candidates:

Bretheren Volunteer Service, sponsored by the
Church of the Bretheren (1451 Dundee Avenue,
Elgin, IL 60120) has two programs lasting four weeks
each, and a special eight-day orientation.
The Chicago Cluster of Theological Schools (1100
East 55th Street, Chicago, IL 60615) conducts an an-
nual mission institute with speakers and leaders from
all religious groups.
The University of Notre Dame's African Studies Pro-

gram (Memorial Library, Notre Dame, IN 46556) is also mission-oriented. It has a program that lasts four weeks.

The Secretariat for Latin America of the National Conference of Catholic Bishops (1312 Massachusetts Avenue NW, Washington, DC 20005) conducts two programs a year aimed at training missionaries to go to Latin America.

The Maryknoll Mission Institute (Maryknoll, NY 10545) conducts several programs every year for missionaries and candidates with special interests and needs. It is open to men and women of all faiths and cultures.

The Mennonite Central Committee (21 South 12th Street, Akron, PA 17501) conducts institutes for Mennonites assigned to overseas work.

The Missionary Internship Program (Box 457, Farmington, MI 48024) has several programs each year for the training of both new missionaries and those home on furlough. Prefield orientation and language acquisition are its specialities.

The Presbyterian Church in the U.S. (341 Ponce de Leon Avenue NE, Atlanta, GA 30308) has annual overseas training programs open to persons of all denominations, space permitting.

The Overseas Ministries Study Center (Ventnor, NJ 08406) is an institution that the prospective candidate for missionary work will want to get acquainted with. It runs year-long conferences on mission work and its various aspects, provides housing for some missionaries on furlough, and is a center for mission research and writing.

The Catholic Theological Union (5401 South Cornell

Avenue, Chicago, IL 60615) provides ecumenical courses in cross-cultural perspectives that would be of interest to overseas career candidates.

The Summer Institute of International Studies (P.O. Box 3117, Fullerton, CA 92634) has a six-week study program at the University of Colorado designed to give perspective to missionaries.

Wheaton College (Summer Institute of Missions, Wheaton, IL 60187) has a two-week summer program which provides advanced training for missionaries and other workers.

There are other groups that have overseas training programs. Both can be investigated through the two intergroup agencies listed above, MARC, or Intercristo. In addition, many colleges and Bible institutes have special programs that should be considered when one is preparing for overseas work.

6

Part-Time, Seasonal, Volunteer, and Independent Careers

A survey of careers in religion reveals thousands of opportunities in places we would expect: local churches, denominations, councils, organizations, and international operations. But there is a vast world of more unusual job possibilities also. These are harder to discover and they require a more imaginative approach to career planning. But there are unlimited opportunities in this miscellaneous category of part-time, seasonal, volunteer, and independent or self-employed careers. Some of these are one of a kind, but to the imaginative, creative person they offer exciting possibilities.

VOLUNTEERS

Volunteer work may not seem as if it should be classified as a career, but for many reasons, we think it should. There are volunteers at every level of religious work, of course, from the church usher and Sunday

194

School teacher on the local level, to the director of a national finance campaign for a denomination, or a member of a national or international church board. All are volunteers, persons serving without pay as part of their stewardship of time and talent.

The kind of volunteer work we are talking about here, however, is of a more organized nature. Many of the national operations of denominations and non church-related organizations discussed in chapters 2 through 6 have extensive volunteer programs which account for much of their personnel.

Churches

The United Presbyterian Church in the USA has a large program called Volunteers in Mission (VIM). It will be used here as an example of what volunteer work is available through the various denominations.

The Volunteers in Mission literature lists several areas of service which are open to qualified personnel. Many of these assignments are for short periods of time—a few weeks or months—although some last as long as a year, or even two or three, with the length of time dependent on the type of work needed. In most cases volunteers receive room and board, a travel allowance, and sometimes a small stipend. Although these are meant to be volunteer programs rather than career assignments, some people with other means of support have made a career of their volunteer assignments. For the average person, volunteer work means investing a portion of one's life in a religious occupation, sometimes in preparation for full-time service later, but often in mid-career or at the time of retirement.

These are some of the opportunities listed in the annual service bulletin of VIM:

• Overseas education service: usually teaching in church-sponsored institutions, and usually overseas (a two-year assignment).

• Other international opportunities for people with special vocational skills: These require a two–three year commitment and a briefing course prior to leaving the country.

• Medical voluntary service: Physicians, nurses, dentists, and other medically related persons are needed, usually for very short-term assignments (some overseas, some in the U.S.).

• Young adult program workers: Persons between the ages of seventeen and twenty-five are needed for a variety of special assignments in churches and community work. Living stipends are usually available.

• National parks ministry: This ecumenical project is also discussed in chapter 3. The work involves a secular park job in addition to off-hours and week-end assignments involving the religious services carried on in the parks.

• Short-term work camps: Many of these are summer assignments for young people, but others are year-round opportunities in all parts of the country.

More information on these kinds of full-time, subsistence-level volunteer programs is available from denominational headquarters (see Appendix C).

Catholic volunteer work is coordinated under the national leadership of the International Liaison, U.S. Catholic Coordinating Center for Lay Volunteer Ministries, 1234 Massachusetts Avenue NE, Suite 1002, Washington, DC 20005. This office's purpose is to "promote, recruit, and develop the concept of the lay missioner both at home and in the foreign field." The International Liaison helps to provide mission placement for hundreds of American Catholics involved in a variety of areas such as catechists, teachers, lay ministers, carpenters, doctors, secretaries, nurses, agronomists, and many other trades and professions. The majority of these placements are from one to three years. In addition, there are some short-term summer placements available.

The International Liaison also publishes an annual list of volunteer service opportunities in a book, *The Response*, which can be ordered from the address above. There are hundreds of openings listed, as well as information about orientation programs, lay missionary organizations in various countries, and other pertinent facts.

Other Volunteer Agencies

There are several non-church agencies, many of them with religious opportunities, that specialize in placing volunteers. Perhaps the best known of these is the Christian Service Corps (CSC), at 1508 Sixteenth Street NW, Washington, DC 20036. This agency and its program are a good example of the type of volunteer opportunities available today. Christian Service Corps is both a placement service and a missionary-sending agency whose workers are "on loan" to mission boards and agencies around the world. CSC recruits skilled personnel for missions. The period of service is usually two years. Many times these volunteers elect to remain with the mission in a full-time career capacity after completing their terms under CSC. CSC also provides a training program which helps make the volunteers ready for service and increases their efficiency. This volunteer program operates under the philosophy that the service being given is on a sacrificial level. Board and room, travel and personal expenses, and fringe benefits of employment are covered, as well as training costs and emergency contingencies. The missions served usually give some financial compensation as well. The total term of service, with training, is usually thirty months. Personnel needs of this organization include a wide variety of occupations. Full information about the program, training opportunities, and possible placement is available from the Christian Service Corps' Washington address.

Coordinating Agencies

On an interdenominational and interagency level, several churches and other groups combine their efforts at recruiting volunteers through the Commission on Voluntary Service and Action. This agency began in 1945 as a coordinating group that set up work camps to help rebuild war-torn Europe. It has since expanded, and coordinates volunteer agencies and agencies placing volunteers. This commission also works closely with national volunteer groups such as the Association of Volunteer Bureaus of America (P.O. Box 7258, Kansas City, MO 64113) and the National Center for Voluntary Action, which has local offices, Voluntary Action Centers, in more than three hundred communities in the U.S.

The Commission on Voluntary Service and Action

publishes an annual listing of work opportunities, *Invest Yourself,* which is available for purchase from the Circulation Manager, 418 Peltoma Road, Haddonfield, NJ 08033, or from the coordinator of CVSA activities, Reverend J. Wilbur Patterson, United Presbyterian Church, 475 Riverside Drive (Room 1126), New York, NY 10027. The 1979 issue of *Invest Yourself* lists opportunities for service in projects sponsored by nearly one hundred agencies and churches. They demonstrate the wide variety of opportunities available and skills needed: geriatrics, agriculture, arts and drama, business and office work, children and youth, community service, counseling, maintenance, health care, legal, work with the handicapped, religious ministry, organizing, teaching, and trade skills.

As we already stated, one of the reasons for discussing volunteer work here, even though it does not usually constitute a career, is that very often a career develops during the time spent in volunteer assignment. This point of view is discussed in detail on a general level in a book by Charlotte Lobb, *Exploring Careers through Volunteerism* (New York: Richards Rosen Press, 1976). Mrs. Lobb makes the point that not only does volunteer work acquaint one with a career, but it also provides training and experience that can be applied later in another related field, or listed on a résumé. In addition, the volunteer gets to know persons involved in his or her chosen field who can later be used as references or to give leads on full-time work. Since there is such an abundance of volunteer work in the religious field, the person considering a career in religion ought to seize every opportunity to investigate, and if possible participate in, some kind of volunteer activity.

PART-TIME AND SEASONAL WORK

In the part-time category there are also many opportunities available through churches and religious organizations. For example, a small church may not be able
to hire a full-time secretary, but may desperately need
someone to work half-time. Such a job could be the
beginning of a career. As other needs develop in the
church, those already employed will be called upon to
increase their duties, and thus eventually may become
full-time workers.

This experience can be duplicated on every level of
work described in this book. Denominational agencies
and their many institutions use part-time or freelance
workers at all professional levels. Some personnel are
needed only on certain days of the week, or at certain
times of year (as accountants, for example). As we will
see later on in this chapter, many persons with the
kinds of skills needed in religious work are making
careers "on their own" by consolidating several part-
time or seasonal opportunities.

Some religious programs, of course, are destined always to be seasonal. Consider, for instance, camping
programs, which in most parts of the country multiply
in the summer, not only because of climatic conditions,
but also because it is vacation time for the children.
Counselors, craft workers, and other specialists—sometimes even camp directors—have other positions, such
as school teachers, in the winter months. Church musicians who need to supplement their salaries often find
employment in a summer music camp or another summer school where special musical training is offered.
Many people who have decided to spend a summer at a

religious camp have been led through that experience into a religious career in camping or some allied pursuit.

The person interested in a seasonal approach to religious careers should examine carefully the many opportunities of this kind listed in the *Directory of Christian Work Opportunities* published by Intercristo or the lists of "volunteer" programs, many of which pay regular salaries for the short term, but list their placements under this broader category.

INDEPENDENT CAREERS

This section of the chapter, on independent careers, might well be entitled "On Your Own," for this is the kind of religious career that we are describing here. Many—there are several hundred such persons—are making their own careers in the religious world. These pursuits are related to religion and are as varied as the people who have developed them.

Many people are making a career of writing, since there are dozens of areas of the church and related religious organizations that require the services of writers, but many of these are not full time. Thus the free-lance writer has come into being in the religious world also. An example of one such person is given later in this chapter.

Other people are using skills they have developed that are needed both in and out of the religious world. Artists are working as free-lance designers and as illustrators of books and materials. Some are doing this full time, as a career. Others are pursuing specialized artistic careers, such as stained glass design and manufacture. One person we talked to in doing research for this book makes his living repairing stained glass church windows all over the country. Since few people have such a skill, he is widely in demand.

Some persons are making a living serving as tour guides or travel agents for religious tours to those parts of the world with religious interest and history. Others are running bookstores or gift shops that specialize in religious materials. Some are working as photographers, developing a career photographing religious subjects.

One could go on almost indefinitely listing the various pursuits in which persons have found religious careers on their own. Many of these people were initially employed by a church or religious agency, but have felt the need for a wider application of their talents or have been inspired to do more creative work under their own auspices. Perhaps the best way to try to get a picture of this is to look at individual experiences and to let some of these people speak for themselves. The following eight examples are people who are "on their own," who have religious careers they themselves have developed.

A Writer

William Coleman of Aurora, Nebraska is a free-lance author who describes his experiences this way:

"The fires started burning again in college. I had decided to give up my dream of writing so I could go into the ministry. Then one day an English professor wrote a note on one of my papers: 'With a little work this could be published.' It was like a match falling on dry leaves.

"Before I left college I had published two articles and I was hooked. For years I pelted the post office with articles. They added up. One day I realized I had published over one hundred articles in twenty-five magazines. The money wasn't much (twenty-five dollars here, seventy-five dollars there), but I was a professional writer, and no one could change that.

"Soon articles were being reprinted. Some magazines had audiences of a quarter million. It was more people than I could reach any other way. Occasionally I'd get mail from someone who was helped. . . .

"Beyond any doubt the biggest problem in a writing career is discouragement. I sent some articles out a dozen times before I sold them. One magazine refused to buy articles for two years. However, eventually that magazine and others were asking me for articles. My byline was appearing in: *Christianity Today, Faith and Inspiration, Moody Monthly, Eternity, Christian Reader,* and *Evangelical Beacon.*

"Most people I talk to about writing fall into one of three classes: those who dream about writing, those who talk about writing, and those who write. If people spent as much time writing as I do they would publish just as often.

"Discouragement is the greatest problem in writing. A person tries once, twice, three times, and quits.

"When first starting out, try to write practically anything for anybody. I have written dozens of book reviews just for the experience. I found one small magazine which had no book review editor, so I volunteered. Every month I wrote the column free of charge. I got to keep the books and gained mountains of experience in paring down material.

"In one town I paid to print a weekly column in the newspaper. Another town gave me the space gratis. Today I write a monthly column for a magazine and *they pay me.* It was worth waiting for.

203

"As with most article writers, the bug to author a book finally bit me. I dabbled at it but was discouraged easily. If one or two publishers rejected the material, I gave up. Rejection is a part of writing. I still don't enjoy it. . . .

"It has been three years since the first book came out. Today I have written ten books, and I am preparing to write a novel."

A Counselor

Art Greer of Houston, Texas, is a counselor in trained transactional analysis with a heavy religious emphasis. This is how Art describes his career:

"In 1970 I had served in churches for five years, as an Air Force chaplain for ten, and as a campus minister for one. I had degrees which all centered around doing therapy/counseling: a BA in philosophy/psychology, a Master of Divinity in the psychology of religion, and a Master of Education in learning theories and educational psychology. The majority of my ministry had centered around counseling. In 1971 I came across transactional analysis (TA) and was so delighted with it as a tool that I received all the training I could get and became certified.

"I began doing lectures and workshops in the field. People began asking me to meet with them, and it soon became necessary to reduce my salaried work by one-half to accommodate them (at a fee!). By 1974 I had been certified by the American Association of Marriage and Family Therapists, and was fairly well known as a TA authority. This, and some great serendipity, led to the writing of my first book (*No Grown-ups in Heaven*) and the decision to leave my other work and go into private practice. Simultaneous to all this, businesses began asking me to do workshops and training seminars for their managers. By 1976, my practice was full-blown and I began to receive invitations to travel for workshops, lectures, and therapy-marathons. In 1978, my second book, *The Sacred Cows Are Dying*, was published.

"At the present time, then, I am doing my private practice of psychotherapy with individuals, groups, and for marriage and family problems. I consult, and do workshops when hired. I preach when asked, and am serving (without charge) as the national program consultant for the Palmer Drug Abuse Program, training staff and working with parents of drug-abusers.

"I see my forte as having expertise in the interface between psychology and religion, and probably do more preaching now than when I was active in the organized ministry, although it frequently doesn't look or sound that way."

Estate Planner

Robert Grunow of Longwood, Florida, has business cards that give his occupation as "Charitable Estate Planning Development Consultant." This rather cumbersome title is explained this way by its owner:

"I have a ministry to the wealthy—perhaps the most misunderstood group in the Christian world! They are a group who need and want a Christian ministry. But they are often neglected and forgotten except when money is needed.

"Jesus often spoke about wealth, riches, and those who had possessions. It has been said that fully one-fourth of all the verses in the Gospels quoting our Lord are about the wealthy—e.g., The Rich Farmer, The Rich Young Ruler, Nicodemus, Zachaeus, and a 'Camel through the eye of a needle.' Christ was most conscious of this group—and so should we be.

"For fifteen years my ministry has been to the wealthy—those whom the Lord has entrusted with hundreds of thousands and millions of dollars.

"How did I get started in this work? Without realizing it, I believe this ministry to the wealthy started before I entered the full-time work for the church. In my early life and in my pastoral ministry, I and my family followed the biblical example of stewardship and I taught members of the congregations I served to do the same. As a result we were successful in raising the level of giving in these churches.

"Apparently officials of the church noted our example and I was 'called' to be a professor at our seminary to teach seminarians to minister to their members—and themselves—in stewardship. At the seminary I was also asked to head up 'fund raising' programs. We were so successful that other institutions, organizations, and congregations asked me to help them as a consultant. Six years ago I resigned my professorship and offered my services as a consultant.

"However, I was not satisfied simply with fund raising. Earlier, as a professor at the seminary, I met Robert Sharpe, now of Memphis, Tennessee, who came to my office and talked to me about charitable estate planning. He invited me to come to his first seminar free of charge—and I did. This started me on what I consider a most exciting ministry to the wealthy.

"The charitable estate plan 'revocable' concept offers the Christian who realizes everything he has is a gift of God the opportunity provided by the Congress of the

United States, through the Internal Revenue Service and the Church foundation, to 1) avoid all possible federal estate taxes and other terminal expenses, 2) provide generously for one's loved ones, and 3) present to the Lord some or all of that which God has entrusted to him.

"Through one's lawyer the Christian steward enters into a revocable, *inter vivos* (living) trust, making himself the trustee. Actually he gives nothing away, keeping full control of all his assets as long as he lives.

"In the living trust, the Christian couple may provide that upon their death, their child, a bank, the administrator of their favorite charity, an official of the church, or any one of their choosing may become the successor trustee to gather some or all of their assets and place them into a church trust, irrevocably.

"Every cent in a church trust will generate a life income for loved ones. Children, for example, may live about thirty years after their parents. This means that if the church trust continues to earn 8 percent interest, over the years children could receive from their parents almost three times what they could have received in a lump sum upon the parents' death. One of the best gestures of the revocable concept is that when the children die, the original amount is still available for the charitable or religious work for which it was given.

"For me this is a fulfilling ministry. I am thankful for the fifteen years I have been able to spend in charitable estate planning."

A Special Ministry

Robert Nugent is a Roman Catholic priest, and Jeannine Grammick, a Catholic Sister. They have established a ministry to homosexuals in the Baltimore, Maryland, area, and it extends to other parts of the country.

Although these two are members of a religious order, theirs is a ministry that could be carried on by unordained personnel.

They call their operation "New Ways Ministry," and explain it thus:

"In 1976 the American Catholic bishops, speaking of the church's ministry to homosexuals, stated that the Christian community should provide for them a special degree of pastoral understanding and care. New Ways Ministry is one small attempt to fulfill this mandate and to respond to a segment of our church and society that has been too long misunderstood and neglected by the mainstream ministries.

"Although both of the codirectors of New Ways have been involved in a ministry to homosexuals since 1971 along with parochial and teaching ministries, we decided formally to collaborate in a more structured way in the spring of 1978. At that time we both experienced increasing requests from individuals and groups for workshops, counseling, retreats, and information on homosexuality, especially in areas involving religion and values. The topic was in the air and even church people were becoming aware of the need to address the question from many perspectives.

"We are an independent and self-supporting ministry with a broad ecumenical outreach. This position provides us with a certain freedom to explore the ministry in ways that the institutional churches are not always comfortable with, such as mixing freely in the gay community and listening to the experiences of gay

Christians, which we feel is crucial to the realization that ministry is a two-way street.

"We have also tried to respond to the church's repeated insistence on the part that social justice plays in proclaiming the gospel, and so we find ourselves in the heart of the struggle for gay rights in a number of areas, including protective legislation and the removal of outdated laws which are unfairly applied and used as means to harass homosexual persons.

"At the present time there are only two of us working in the ministry but we are fortunate enough to have several volunteers who share our concern and are willing to lend a hand when it comes time to mail out information. We are both a nonprofit and tax-exempt incorporated organization and use the stipends and workshop fees to support the overhead expenses of New Ways. We depend on donations from people who support our ministry.

"One of our major projects at the present time and one which also enables us to pay one full-time and one part-time salary is a study on the 'coming out' process and coping strategies of gay women. The project is sponsored by the San Diego chapter of Dignity, Inc. and funded by the Department of Health, Education and Welfare.

"We also do retreats and days of prayer for various gay groups throughout the United States and Canada, as well as individual talks and workshops for nongay groups such as counselors, teachers, pastors, social workers, etc. This one-day workshop model has been most successful especially for people who have little or no knowledge of homosexuality. While there have been some rough spots along the way with nervous church officials of far-right groups, we have found for the most part both encouragement and interest from our co-religionists who see the need for this vital ministry. It is a new and unexplored ministry and we proceed step by step into uncharted waters."

A Home for Special Children

Dorothy Gauchat is president of the board of trustees and director of Our Lady of the Wayside, Inc., a residential home for mentally retarded and physically handicapped children. This very effective ministry grew out of the personal experience of Dorothy and her husband, Bill, who began early in their married life to care in their home for children whom others had considered "hopeless." Through the love that they and their own six children showered on these foster children, some "miracles" happened. Eventually the Gauchats bought a farm to house more children. Finally they built a home especially designed for this special care, even though they maintained the special family atmosphere with a heavy religious emphasis that made their care so effective. The Wayside has become a major institution in Avon, Ohio, a suburb of Cleveland. It is an independent operation with a board of advisors from the medical and ecumenical religious leadership of the community. Since her husband's untimely death, Mrs. Gauchat has been in charge of the home. She wrote of her experiences in a book, *All God's Children*, published in 1976 by Hawthorn Books. In the final chapter of the book Dorothy Gauchat describes her struggles in building the home. She ends her book with these words:

At last we dedicated our new home. It was beautiful, nestled among the trees overlooking the lake. It was alive with color and music and filled with friends who had helped build it for God's children.

Above all, it was filled with children, who carried their toys and clothes from the old house and put them carefully in the new closets and drawers. Finally, the children cut the red ribbon stretched across the entrance and sent hundreds of balloons heavenward to praise and thank God. We called this new home Our Lady of the Wayside.

A Teacher of Teachers

Locke Bowman of Scottdale, Arizona, is a Presbyterian minister with a very special career. Although he is a clergyman, his teaching ministry could be run by an unordained person. After several years spent in the parish ministry and later in the education office of his denomination, Locke decided to specialize in what he had found to be his speciality: teaching teachers of religion. With some foundation funds that helped him get started, he established the National Teacher Education Project (NTEP), which has blossomed into a large ministry employing several people.

NTEP has a year-round schedule of teaching institutes utilizing the best modern equipment and teaching techniques to train religious teachers of all denominations. The sessions usually last one week and concentrate on the study of the best skills that can be offered. Recently the staff of NTEP has also been conducting shorter sessions lasting two or three days called TIPS, which stands for Teacher Improvement: Practice/Study.

In addition to these special teaching sessions, NTEP conducts media production workshops to help teachers learn to use the many modern teaching media available. A few years ago Locke Bowman began publishing a monthly magazine, *Church Teachers*, in order to continue the ministry that begins with teachers in the training sessions. NTEP also produces cassettes for self-instruction, and teaching without a teacher, as well as many other kinds of materials that they produce themselves or buy from other publishers and producers and distribute to their teachers.

Media Specialist

In Pittsburgh, Pennsylvania, there is another Presbyterian who has a career similar in many respects to that of Locke Bowman, but with quite a different emphasis and outreach. Dennis Benson is a virtual dynamo, so bursting with ideas that simply trying to list what he does is impossible. He may not be doing tomorrow what he is doing today. Nevertheless, here is a sampling of this man's work.

Dennis has the ability to reach lives, especially those of young people, with decision-making precision, and to influence them to invest themselves in God-directed activities. In the process he also uses all of the techniques of the modern world and harnesses current ideas to productive uses. For example, nine times a year Dennis publishes a newspaper called *Scan*. It is sent to a large list of persons involved in religious pursuits—especially educators—who in turn are reaching others. This publication is billed as "A forum for the creative review of the best in print, electric and human resources." In this publication Dennis discusses many of his own books, as well as materials that have been produced by some of the major religious houses, but he also ferrets out the many new and unusual publications on the market or are about to be. He also publishes a paper called *Recycle*, which capitalizes on the current interest in recycling both products and lives.

As word about him has spread, Dennis and his friends have been invited to give speeches, lead groups, and conduct workshops for church and community leaders on Dennis's ideas. He has literally traveled around the world with his "recycle theology workshops," and his ideas multiply each time he speaks to a new group.

Besides the books that he continues to write and have published, Dennis also produces programs for radio and TV both in his area and for other outlets. In all of his activities, Dennis is in touch with theological changes and activities and action both inside and outside the church. He embodies within himself and his work many of the renewal efforts that have made the Christian message come alive in the latter days of the twentieth century.

Advertising Manager

Ruth Taylor of Scarsdale, New York, carved out for herself an unusual career in religion. After her children were grown, Ruth went to work as an advertising manager for a small religious magazine. Thus she came to know the many other religious magazines that could not afford an advertising manager, but needed the kind of services that she could provide part time. She describes her experience thus:

"My career in advertising management started in

1961 when I was asked to help out as advertising manager for *The National Lutheran*, a house organ of the Lutheran Council. Although I had an M.S. degree in industrial psychology, which included some study of advertising, I was completely green about setting up an advertising program, and had to start from the ground up. I was encouraged to take the job, however, because I knew the Lutheran church and its background well and felt this would compensate for my lack of experience in advertising management. Two experienced secretaries in the office helped me set up an excellent system for processing advertising orders, which I continue to use today.

"Fortunately I was quite successful both in procuring the quota of ads needed, and keeping office procedures in good order. Therefore, some of the people on the council's Board of Directors, who were also on the boards of other church-affiliated publications, recommended me as an advertising manager. Eventually I was asked if I would also serve in this capacity for other publications. I began then to do most of the advertising solicitation by phone from my home, and to call on clients and work at the publication offices only when necessary.

"Over the past eighteen years, I have been the advertising manager for nineteen publications, representing Catholic, Protestant, and nondenominational publications. Presently I am serving ten. This keeps me busy full time, and from time to time, in busy seasons, means hiring part-time help. It is a satisfying and challenging career that just happened in my life."

Appendixes

The appendixes on the following pages will be help-ful to persons considering careers in religion:

Appendix A: A Listing of Church Occupations

Lists fifty-four occupations in eight categories, giving activities involved and training required

Appendix B: College Majors and Careers in Religion

Gives twenty-nine college majors matched with the careers in religion for which they are preparation

Appendix C: Denominational Career Offices

Tells whom to contact in twenty national church bodies for help in planning a career in religion

Appendix D: Church Career Development Centers

Lists career counseling services in fourteen locations in the United States

Appendix E: Other Resources

Lists books, pamphlets, and brochures that will help in the search for a religious career

Appendix A: A Listing of Church Occupations

The following extensive listing of church occupations, the activities involved, and the training requirements for each of them, is based on *A Listing of Church Occupations*, published in 1977 by the Office of Professional Church Leadership of the National Council of Churches of Christ in the U.S.A., 475 Riverside Drive, New York, NY 10027, and is used with their permission.

Although these are listed as "church" occupations, most of them could be duplicated in the programs of non church-related religious organizations and institutions as well. Users of this book will also note that occupations requiring ordination are also included. However, the vast majority of these occupations are for the unordained.

OCCUPATIONS	ACTIVITIES	TRAINING REQUIREMENTS
I. Local Church		
1. Pastor–Local Church	Administers the sacraments; preaches; calls; counsels; teaches, coordinates program.	Academic preparation: usually seven years of study beyond high school. B.A. or its equivalent plus Master of Divinity and denominational ordination.
2. Associate or Assistant Pastor or Minister of Education	Most duties listed above; special responsibilities assigned such as leadership training, program coordination education, group work, visitation.	Academic preparation: usually seven years of study beyond high school. A B.A. or its equivalent plus Master of Divinity and denominational ordination.
3. Minister of Music	Role of music in all phases of the church's life. Multiple staff relationships.	Basic training for ordination plus required courses in church music.
4. Director of Music	Directs one or more choirs; plans music programs; may serve as organist.	Bachelor's degree with major in music and additional required courses in church music.
5. Counseling Pastor	Conducts individual group counseling; attached to a local church staff or a counseling center.	Basic training for ordination plus advance degrees in psychology and related subjects.
6. Director of Christian Education	Directs total educational program; does teacher training; gives leadership and counsel to all age groups in the local church.	Master's degree in Christian education. Certified after fulfilling requirements of denomination which includes several years of experience.
7. Educational Associate or Assistant for special groups—children—young adults—handicapped	Directs designated groups in study; planning, worship, recreation. Recruits; trains; and supervises volunteers.	Bachelor's degree with major in Christian education in special field, or its equivalent.

OCCUPATIONS	ACTIVITIES	TRAINING REQUIREMENTS
8. Director or Teacher weekday church school	Supervises and/or teaches courses in religion on released time and after school.	Bachelor's degree, major in Bible and Christian education. Director often required to have Master's degree and certification by the State Board of Education.
9. Director or Teacher of Nursery School or Kindergarten	Organizes and supervises program; recruits teachers; teaches pre-school children.	Bachelor's degree with major in early childhood education. Certification necessary for supervisor.
10. Lay Pastor or Reader	Preaches; in some denominations serves as pastor to small church without authorization to administer sacraments.	Usually college degree or its equivalent plus special training by correspondence and summer school.
11. Church Custodian (Full Time)	Keeps church and parish buildings clean, orderly, ventilated, heated; arranges furniture and equipment; cooperates with staff.	Building engineer skills in heating, lighting, plumbing, and cleaning; devotion to the church; understanding of people.
II. Education: Colleges and Universities		
12. College or Prep School Professor or Teacher	Teaches, administers, counsels, does research related to courses presented.	A minimum of Master's degree for beginning positions; a Ph.D. (except for dissertation) required by many schools. Full professor must have Ph.D.
13. Professor in Theological School	Similar to activities in general teaching program specializing in church history, Biblical subjects, church polity and doctrine.	Master of Divinity plus Ph.D. or Th.D. in area of teaching.

219

OCCUPATIONS	ACTIVITIES	TRAINING REQUIREMENTS
14. Campus Minister	Serves as pastor to academic community, usually on a coordinated religious staff, may teach religion courses.	Master of Divinity plus additional training for campus ministry; pastoral experience is advisable; often hired by and serving several denominations.
15. Campus Religious Coordinator	Coordinates and supervises total program of campus ministry; often teaches courses in religions and related subjects.	Basic training for ordination; a doctorate with special concern for religion in higher education; hired by the college or university.
16. Assistant Religious Coordinator	Assists Religious Coordinator in program activities; group work, projects, music, recreation, and personal counseling.	Bachelor's degree, post graduate study in religion, leadership training and counseling.
17. Guidance Counselor or Placement Officer	Counsels concerning occupational choice; gives and interprets tests; coordinates interviews between students and prospective employees.	Master's degree plus advanced work in guidance, counseling, and business administration.
18. Librarian	Organizes; supervises; purchases; catalogues; circulates books, magazines, films, tapes; does research, writes book reviews.	Master's in library science plus additional preparation according to the size of institution and position.
III. Health and Welfare Institutions		
19. Administrator of Hospital or Home	Supervises institution; develops policy; raises money, works with Board of Trustees.	Bachelor's in business administration plus Master's in hospital administration or advanced studies related to the position.
20. Supervisor in Hospital or Home	Supervises office staff or hospital or home; manages property, and coordinates public relations.	Bachelor's in administration with Master's in hospital administration.

220

OCCUPATIONS	ACTIVITIES	TRAINING REQUIREMENTS
21. Medical Technologist	Member of medical team; makes laboratory tests to help in diagnosis and treatment of disease.	Three years of college and one year of directed study.
22. Medical X-ray Technician	Uses X-ray equipment for diagnostic and therapeutic treatment of patients.	Junior college diploma plus twenty-four months of training in hospital affiliated with a medical school.
23. Nurse (Registered)	Provides general staff nursing services; supervises; teaches allied nursing personnel; serves in hospitals, schools, or as a visiting nurse.	Three year hospital school of nursing, or four or five year college degree course with major in nursing. State license required.
24. Occupational Therapist	Follows physician's instructions; selects and directs educational, occupational, and recreation activities of patients.	Degree in occupational therapy from a school approved by the American Medical Association.
25. Physical Therapist	Follows physician's instructions; treats a variety of disorders through physical exercises; uses mechanical apparatuses as well as massage, heat, light, water, electricity.	Four year course in physical therapy, or a one to two year course after bachelor's degree plus state examination for certification.
26. Physician	Diagnoses diseases and treats people in office and in hospital. Concerned with preventive medicine and rehabilitation.	Graduate from approved medical school; passes a state licensing exam and serves one or more years as hospital intern.
27. Medical Records Librarian	Organizes and keeps medical records of patients; does research for doctors and hospital staff.	Two years of college or graduate of nursing school plus one year's training in medical library systems.
28. Dietitian	Plans meals in hospitals, aging and children's homes, church headquarters, and large churches; supervises staff; purchases supplies and equipment; keeps records.	Bachelor's degree from accredited school with special studies in food and nutrition or equivalent. One year's internship required for accreditation.
29. Hospital Attendant	Assists patients in bathing, eating, dressing, walking; makes beds; cleans rooms; carries trays.	High school diploma preferred; advancement depends on willingness to attend training programs.

OCCUPATIONS	ACTIVITIES	TRAINING REQUIREMENTS
30. House Parents or Resident Director	Guides, inspires, instructs, loves the occupants of their home as a parent.	Mature person who understands and loves children and is accepted by them. College courses in child psychology helpful.
IV. Chaplaincy		
31. Chaplain-Military	Serve as pastor to personnel in military forces.	Ordained minister who has served two or more years in a local church plus accreditation given by denomination; required to attend chaplain's school after acceptance by a branch of service.
32. Institutional Chaplain (Hospital-Home-Prison-Industry)	Serves as religious counselor; visits; conducts worship; relates to management and persons served.	Ordained; clinical and specialized training for type of institution.
V. Missional Outreach		
33. Missionary (Global or National) No one OOH number is given; check specific occupation for missionary interest	Pioneers, experiments, enables mission through expertise in given occupation; education, evangelism, medicine, social service, relief work, agriculture, community organizer and others as needed.	College degree and/or training in occupation. Commissioned by a church board to fill a request for an indigenous church or institution.
34. Short Career Service Term No one OOH number is given; check specific occupation for missionary interest	Trained and experienced in dentistry, surgery, carpentry, agriculture, etc. Serves from three months to a year to fulfill a specific function requested by a church or institution.	Must be a highly competent professional, giving time and often furnishing supplies and expenses.

OCCUPATIONS	ACTIVITIES	TRAINING REQUIREMENTS
35. Director/Manager Church Camp	Coordinates and develops program; directs public relations; trains camp leaders; manages the facilities.	Master's degree, with major in program development, leadership training, human relations and property management. Theological training helpful but not required.
36. Deaconess	A woman selected, trained and commissioned to work in any of the ministries of the church related to teaching, healing, social welfare in rural and urban, and local church.	Bachelor's degree with graduate study in speciality. One year's experience in the field under supervision before being commissioned.
37. Evangelist	Similar to pastor, on occasion conducts special preaching services for one or more churches; supervises every member visitation; and compliments work of local pastor.	Basic training for ordination plus interest in evangelism, Master of Divinity or its equivalent.
38. Social Worker	Interviews; counsels individuals and groups to discover their needs and to assist in the solving of the problems discovered; works in settlement houses, mission stations, and inner-city churches; cooperates with social and welfare agencies.	Master's in Social Science or its equivalent with major in any one of many specialities needed in social work.
39. Community Center Worker (Club organizer, recreation, crafts, counselor)	Caring, serving and sharing presence to help solve problems, including poverty, broken homes, emotional handicaps, antisocial behavior; in neighborhood centers, inner-city or rural projects.	Bachelor's degree with major in human relations, counseling, program planning and leadership training.
40. Director of Social Service	Supervises several community, social and welfare agencies; often serves as representative of denomination or Council of Churches to city administration and the courts.	Master's degree in Social Science with advanced courses in human relations; ordination helpful but not required.

223

OCCUPATIONS	ACTIVITIES	TRAINING REQUIREMENTS
41. Relief Worker	Distributes clothing and food; organizes community action; cooperates with governmental agencies.	College degree or equivalent with knowledge of language and customs of people.
VI. Business Administration		
42. Accountant	Compiles and analyzes financial records; prepares necessary reports for national and regional offices; can be related to hospitals, homes, universities and colleges.	Bachelor's degree with major in accounting; additional study related to the institution. Certification as a public accountant often necessary.
43. Business Manager	Manages office, property, and personnel; prepares financial reports; directs public relations and stewardship programs in local churches, national or regional offices, universities, colleges and publishing houses.	Degree in business administration or equivalent, plus previous experience in the field.
44. Personnel Worker	Recruits; interviews; tests and evaluates individuals; assists in hiring of new personnel.	Degree in Business Administration or its equivalent; courses in personnel management, labor relations, and economics.
45. Director of Research and Survey	Conducts research related to trends and norms; evaluates areas of need; usually serves in denominational or Council of Churches headquarters.	Special research training beyond Bachelor's degree, with training for ordination helpful but not required.
46. Clerks	Works for boards and agencies in following areas: receiving, stock, packaging, shipping, mailing, sales, files, records, bookkeeping.	High school diploma or equivalent with on the job training.
47. Secretary	Takes dictation; types; operates office machines; files; serves as receptionist.	High school diploma with secretarial training. Business school training for more advanced positions.

OCCUPATIONS	ACTIVITIES	TRAINING REQUIREMENTS
VII. Communication and Media		
48. Director of Audiovisuals	Develops programs and produces them for radio, television and film.	Bachelor's degree plus graduate work in audiovisuals.
49. Director of Public Relations	Promotes public relations via newspaper, radio, television; directs special programs; serves in large churches, Council of Churches, area and regional offices.	Bachelor's degree with major in journalism; proven ability to write and demonstrated skills in specialty.
50. Commercial Artists	Collaborates with editors and other initiators of art work; creates; designs; illustrates; and creates typographical layouts.	Three or four years of formal training in commercial art or a Bachelor's degree with major in art.
51. Publishing House Staff (Manager, Printer, Salesman, Office and Plant Personnel, Bookstore)	Publishes curriculum materials; promotes sales through service centers and bookstores.	Training appropriate to occupation. Many jobs require a college degree with on the job training for others.
52. Editor or Staff Writer	Prepares curriculum for given age groups; writes articles; edits magazines.	Master's degree with proven skills in writing and editing. Theological training helpful but not required.
VIII. Miscellaneous		
53. Denominational or Ecumenical Executive	Supervises; coordinates programs for general or area boards or agencies.	Master's degree, with major in program development, leadership training, human relations. Theological training helpful but not necessary.
54. Building Superintendent (Hospitals, homes, schools, boards, agencies)	Supervises staff for building maintenance depending on size of plant, regulates ventilation, heating, lighting, cleaning and plumbing.	Training as building superintendent plus experience. College degree in engineering helpful.

225

Appendix B: College Majors and Careers in Religion

The following chart is useful for those considering a career in religion as they decide on their college majors. It is also a guide for persons in mid-career contemplating religious work who may already have the background and training that would qualify them for many occupations listed.

This chart published by the Department of Ministry of the National Council of Churches of Christ in the U.S.A., 475 Riverside Drive, New York, NY 10027, in 1968 is reprinted with their permission. A similar chart is published in the annual *Directory of Christian Work Opportunities*, and is available from Intercristo, The International Christian Organization, Box 9323, Seattle, WA 98109.

Your Choice of a Major	Your Career Opportunities
Accounting and Finance	Bookkeeping in religious organizations or agencies.* Fiscal supervision and administration in churches or church-sponsored institution.* Fund management for religious foundations or churches.
Agriculture	Missionary service in agricultural communities.* Rural church ministry.* Teaching in the areas of animal husbandry and crop production in church-related agricultural institutions.
Architecture	Architectural consultant services for churches and church-sponsored organizations.*
Art	Design and layout of religious texts and periodicals in a publishing house. Production of audio-visual materials for denominations and councils of churches. Teaching in church-related institutions.*
Biology	Medical and dental work and laboratory research in church-sponsored hospitals, clinics, or schools.* Nutrition and dietetics in mission schools, hospitals, or rest homes.* Teaching in church-related schools and colleges.*

* At home or overseas.

227

Your Choice of a Major

Your Career Opportunities

Business Management

Administration of church-related social or community centers.
Administration of homes for children and homes for the aging.
Administration of large metropolitan or suburban churches.
Executive responsibility in religious foundations and church-related institutions.
Management and sales work for church-related bookstores and publishing houses.
Office management in denominational or church council headquarters.*
Teaching in church-related colleges and universities.*

Drama and Speech

Religious drama production for stage, screen, radio, or television.
Religious motion picture production.
Teaching in church-related colleges and universities.*

Earth Sciences

Research in archaeology.*
Teaching in church-related colleges and universities.*

Economics

Actuarial and investment work for church pension boards.*
Business management in various areas of church operation.*
Teaching in church-related colleges and universities.*

* At home or overseas.

**Your Choice
of a Major**

Your Career Opportunities

Education

Direction of children's, youth, or adult work for regional or national church agencies.

Serving as a teacher or director of Christian education in the local church or council of churches.

Teaching in church weekday preschool programs and in weekday classes of religion for public school pupils.

Teaching or administration of primary or secondary schools as well as colleges and universities.*

Engineering

Development and design of new or expanding church facilities.

Teaching in church-related colleges, universities, and technical schools.

Supervision and maintenance of church buildings, mission stations, hospitals, or campuses of church-related schools and colleges.*

English

Creative writing for church magazines and periodicals.

Editing for church school, fellowship, or other religious books and periodicals.

Serving as religious editor for secular newspapers, magazines, and book publishers.

Teaching in church-related colleges and universities.*

* At home or overseas.

Your Choice of a Major	Your Career Opportunities
Government and Political Science	Executive staff of city, state, or national councils of churches in social action fields. Participation as religious representative in community councils and local government boards. Serving in the secretariats of church world service or other world religious agencies.* Teaching in schools, colleges, and universities.*
History	Preparation of church school curriculum materials. Teaching in church-related schools, colleges, and universities.*
Home Economics	Food management and buying for hospitals, homes, camps, colleges, or other church-related institutions.* Teaching in church-related schools or colleges.*
Journalism	Editing and managing denominational and interdenominational publications. Employment on staff of church publications. Serving as religious editor for a newspaper. Writing news releases and publicity material for churches or religious agencies. Writing religious articles and stories for mass media. * At home or overseas.

Your Choice of a Major	Your Career Opportunities
Languages—Classical and/or Modern	Ministry to non-English-speaking congregations.
	Research and translation in the area of Biblical history and literature.
	Teaching in church-related schools, colleges, universities, and seminaries.*
Library Science	Serving as librarian for church-related colleges and universities.*
	Serving as librarian for denominational headquarters
Mathematics	Administration of denominational pension and retirement programs.
	Computer programming and use in denominational and council headquarters.
	Statistical research for national church offices and agencies.
	Teaching in church-related colleges and universities.*
Music	Choral and musical directing in a local church.
	Composition and performance of music for religious films and filmstrips.
	Production and editing of hymnals and other liturgical materials.
	Serving as organist, instrumentalist, or vocalist in a local church.
	Teaching in church-related schools, colleges, and universities.*
Nursing	Caring for the sick in a church-related hospital.*
	Supervision of training programs in church-related agencies for nurse's aides and other hospital workers.
	Teaching home nursing and child care at mission posts or other church agencies.*

* At home or overseas.

Your Choice of a Major	Your Career Opportunities
Pharmacy	Pharmacist in church-related hospitals or clinics.*
Philosophy and Religion	Educational counseling in local, regional, or national agencies. Teaching in church-related schools, colleges, universities, and seminaries.*
Physical Education, Health, and Recreation	Athletic coaching and physical education instruction in church-related schools, colleges, and universities.* Directing recreational activities in a local YMCA or YWCA or in church-sponsored camps. Serving in church-related community centers. Therapeutic and rehabilitative work in the hospitals, homes, and other agencies of the church.*
Physics and Chemistry	Serving as a scientist or lab technician in church-related hospitals, clinics, and laboratories. Teaching in church-related schools, colleges, and universities.*
Psychology	Chaplaincy in prisons, hospitals, schools, and other institutions. Counseling and/or teaching in a church-related college, university, or seminary.* Counseling in a local church or in a denominational or interdenominational center. Personnel work in denominational or interdenominational centers. Social work in a community center or mission station.*

* At home or overseas.

Your Choice of a Major	Your Career Opportunities
Public Relations and Advertising	Advertising and public relations work for church publishing houses. Church publicity and promotion. Fund raising in local churches, state and national denominational offices, or councils of churches. Promotion of church programs.
Social Work	Church-related work with social welfare agencies in child placement, adult rehabilitation, and family counseling. Church relief and rehabilitation.* Guidance service in the areas of family life and community action. Social work in a church-related community center.*
Sociology	Community research and surveys for denominational agencies or councils of churches relating to church extension and rehabilitation. Counseling ministry to families and communities. Teaching and research in church-related colleges and universities and in seminaries.* * At home or overseas.

Appendix C: Denominational Career Offices

Most denominations have an office to which people may write for information on church occupations. These offices list summer service opportunities, schools and colleges where training is available, financial aid resources, and other helpful information. Some of them publish books and brochures which give specific suggestions to persons of their own denomination.

The following is a list of most of those denominational agencies which have special personnel dealing with career questions:

African Methodist Episcopal
Church
Department of Education
1461 Northgate Road
Washington, DC 20012

African Methodist Episcopal
Zion Church
Christian Education

Department
128 East 58th Street
Chicago, IL 60637

American Baptist Churches
Commission on the Ministry
Valley Forge, PA 19481

The American Lutheran
Church

Office of Support to Ministries
422 South Fifth Street
Minneapolis, MN 55415

Christian Churches (Disciples
of Christ)
Interagency Committee on
Church Vocations
222 South Downey Avenue
Indianapolis, IN 46219

Christian Methodist Episcopal
Church
Board of Christian Education
564 E. Frank Avenue
Memphis, TN 38106

The Church of God
Board of Christian Education
Box 2458
Anderson, IN 46011

Church of the Brethren
1451 Dundee Avenue
Elgin, IL 60120

The Episcopal Church
The Executive Council
815 Second Avenue
New York, NY 10017

Friends United Meeting
Meeting Ministries
Commission
101 Quaker Hill Drive
Richmond, IN 47374

Lutheran Church in America
Division for Professional
Leadership
2900 Queen Lane
Philadelphia, PA 19129

Moravian Church in America,
North

5 West Market Street
Bethlehem, PA 18018

Presbyterian Church in the
U.S.
Division of Court Partnership
Services
341 Ponce de Leon Avenue,
N.E.
Atlanta, GA 30308

Reformed Church in America
Office of Human Resources
475 Riverside Drive
New York, NY 10027

Southern Baptist Convention
Program of Vocational
Guidance
127 Ninth Avenue North
Nashville, TN 37203

United Church of Canada
Board of Colleges
85 St. Clair Avenue, East
Toronto 7, Ontario, Canada

United Church of Christ
Office for Church Life and
Leadership
289 Park Avenue South
New York, NY 10010

United Methodist Church
Office of Personnel
Board of Higher Education and
Ministry
P.O. Box 871
Nashville, TN 37202

United Presbyterian Church,
U.S.A.
Vocation Agency
475 Riverside Drive Rm 432
New York, NY 10027

Roman Catholic Offices
National Sisters Vocation
Conference
1307 South Wabash Avenue
Chicago, IL 60605

National Catholic Vocational
Council
1307 South Wabash Avenue
Chicago, IL 60605

General information on church
occupations can be had by
writing:

Professional Church Leadership
Division of Education and
Ministry
National Council of Churches
475 Riverside Drive, Room 770
New York, NY 10027

Appendix D: Church Career Development Centers

In 1969, fourteen denominations organized a Church Career Development Council to provide special career counseling services to persons in professional leadership positions in the church. The council has also established regional centers throughout the country to make access easier to persons in all parts of the U.S. and Canada. These centers are available for both individual and group career counseling.

Career Development Center
St. Andrews Presbyterian
College
Laurinburg, NC 28352
(919) 276-3162

Career Development Center
Eckerd College
St. Petersburg, FL 33733
(813) 867-1166

Center for the Ministry
7804 Capwell Drive
Oakland, CA 94621
(415) 635-4246

Center for the Ministry
40 Washington Street
Wellesley Hills, MA 02181
(617) 237-2228

Judicatory Career Support
System
3501 Campbell
Kansas City, MO 64109
(816) 931–2516

Lancaster Career Development
Center
561 College Avenue
Lancaster, PA 17604
(717) 397–7451

Mid-South Career
Development Center
1007 18th Avenue South
Nashville, TN 37212
(615) 327–9572

Midwest Career Development
Center
66 East 15th Avenue
Columbus, OH 43201
(614) 294–2587   and
176 Adams Street, Suite 1400
Chicago, IL 60603
(312) 263–2714

New England Career

Development Center
40 Washington Street
Wellesley Hills, MA 02181
(617) 237–2228

North Central Career
Development Center
3000 Fifth Street, NW
New Brighton, MN 55112
(612) 636–5120

Northeast Career Center
291 Witherspoon Street
Princeton, NJ 08540
(609) 924–4814

Southwest Career Development
Center
P.O. Box 5923
Arlington, TX 76011
(817) 265–5541

Western Career Development
Center
127 North Madison Avenue,
Suite 202
Pasadena, CA 91101
(213) 449–6271

Appendix E:
Other Resources

The following list of books, pamphlets, directories, and brochures should be helpful in the search for a religious career.

BROCHURES AND PAMPHLETS

The National Council of Churches, Department of Professional Church Leadership, 475 Riverside Drive, New York, NY 10027, distributes a packet of materials for those interested in vocational guidance. Included in this packet of materials are "What Is a Church Occupation," a six-page pamphlet; "A Listing of Church Occupations" and "College Majors and Careers in the Church" (see Appendixes A and B); "The Christian Ministry: A Challenge," a sixteen-page booklet; and "Financial Aid for Professional and Graduate Education," a twenty-page booklet listing sources of scholarships and grants for training for religious occupations. Write the NCC for prices and other information.

Denominations and national church organizations also publish and distribute helpful publications. Examples of these are a fifty-six-page book, *Church Occupations and Career Planning,* available from the Office of Career Planning and Personnel Services of the United Methodist Board of Higher Education and Ministry, Box 871, Nashville, TN 37202; *You and Your Occupational Choice,* a four-page brochure published by the Vocation Agency of the United Presbyterian Church, 475 Riverside Drive, New York, NY 10027; *Vocational Guidance in a Church,* a one hundred twenty-eight-page paperback study guide published by Convention Press of the Southern Baptist Sunday School Board, 127 Ninth Avenue North, Nashville, TN 37234. Southern Baptists also publish a complete set of two- to four-page vocational guidance brochures on separate vocations. Similar materials are available from other denominations.

Other religious organizations and interchurch agencies also publish brochures and pamphlets which can be obtained by writing to the personnel offices of each of these organizations.

DIRECTORIES

Directory of Christian Work Opportunities, Intercristo, The International Christian Organization, P.O. Box 9323, Seattle, WA 98108. An annual listing of some twenty thousand job openings in six hundred organizations. Listings in three categories: jobs available, agencies, and location. The 1979 directory has 916 pages and sells for $20.

Directory of Religious Organizations, A Consortium Book by McGrath Publishing Co., Wilmington, NC 28401. Brief information on more than 1,000 organizations active in the field of religion. Divided into nine categories: special ministries, spiritual life, teaching and nursing orders, academic and educational, social justice, foreign missions, evangelical, media and professional, and ecumenical. The 1977 edition had 553 pages.

Mission Handbook, North American Protestant Ministries Overseas, edited by Edward R. Dayton. Available from the Mission Advanced Research and Communications Center, 919 Huntington Drive, Monrovia, CA 91016. Published every three years. The most recent edition, the twelfth, was published in 1979. It surveys some seven hundred agencies doing Christian work overseas.

Yearbook of American and Canadian Churches, Constant H. Jacquet, Jr., editor. Prepared by the Office of Research, Evaluation and Planning of the National Council of Churches of Christ in the U.S.A. Published and distributed by Abingdon Press, 201 Eighth Avenue, Nashville, TN 37202. An invaluable source of information on all denominations and religious organizations.

In addition to the interchurch and interagency directories, most larger denominations issue a yearbook or annual which would be an aid to anyone seeking employment within that denomination. Consult the list of church-owned publishing houses in chapter 2, Careers in Church-Wide Institutions and Offices.

Images of Women in Mission, A Resource Guide and Directory of Catholic Church Vocations for Women (1979), edited by Sr. Frances Cunningham; and *Ministries for the Lord, A Resource Guide and Directory of Catholic Church Vocations for*

Men (1978), Paulist Press, New York. These two directories list alphabetically religious orders in the Roman Catholic Church and detail career opportunities in each of them.

BOOKS ON CAREERS IN RELIGION

Careers of Service in the Church, by Benson Y. Landis (New York: Evans and Lippincott, 1964). Good general information on church careers with an alphabetical list by occupation. Emphasis on opportunities in education.

Careers in the Christian Ministry (Wilmington, NC: Consortium Books, 1976). A collection of ecumenical essays on careers in the ordained ministry. General information useful to the unordained career searcher as well.

Careers in Religious Communications, by Roland E. Wolseley (Scottdale, PA: Herald Press, 1977). A new third edition of this popular, comprehensive book by the former director of the department of religious journalism at Syracuse University in New York.

Church Vocations—A New Look, by Murray J. S. Ford (Valley Forge, PA: Judson Press, 1971). A look at church careers both "on location" and "outside the walls." An alphabetical list by occupations. Chapter on experimental ministries especially helpful.

DCE—A Challenging Career in Christian Education, by Louise McComb (Atlanta: John Knox Press, 1963). A good basic book on the work of the Director of Christian Education in the local church.

The D.R.E. Book by Maria Harris (New York: Paulist Press, 1976). More up-to-date and complete coverage than DCE on the many facets of the work of Director of Religious Education. Written from a Catholic point of view but helpful to DREs in all churches.

The Electric Church, by Ben Armstrong (Nashville: Thomas Nelson, 1979). An analysis of the burgeoning field of religion on radio and television.

Minister, Man in the Middle, by John B. Coburn (New York: Macmillan, 1956). Written about the ordained ministry, somewhat outdated but still helpful guide for the career searcher in delineating the varieties of ministries available.

Person and Profession, by Charles W. Stewart (Nashville: Abingdon Press, 1974). Career development in the ministry.

GENERAL BOOKS ON CAREERS

The general category is almost limitless. Many public libraries have established a special section on careers. The following are a few recent titles which have a special application to those thinking about a religious career.

Career Search, A Personal Pursuit, by Edward N. Chapman (Chicago: Science Research Associates, Inc., 1976). A good study of the process of searching for a career in two phases, with ten steps each.

Careers Today, by Gene R. Howes, et al. (New York: New American Library, 1977). A guide to 150 challenging jobs. Chapters on medical and other health care centers touch on religious opportunities.

Creating the Future: A Guide to Living and Working for Social Change, by Charles Beitz and Michael Washburn (New York: Bantam Books, 1974). A guide to opportunities in the field of social change, many relating to religious careers. Shows relationship between work and life styles.

Exploring Careers through Volunteerism, by Charlotte Lobb (New York: Richard Rosen Press, 1976). A guide to using volunteer work to find a career. Useful to those considering volunteer or short-term assignments for religious organizations.

Get Your Career in Gear: How to Find or Change Your Life Work, by John William Zehring (Wheaton, IL: Victor Books, 1976). Information on self-understanding, skills, and job-hunting techniques. Written from a Christian perspective.

How to Get the Job That's Right for You, by Ben Greco (Homewood, IL: Dow Jones-Irwin, 1975). Self-analysis related to job opportunities. The seventy-five pages of appendixes and bibliography are especially helpful.

Job Résumés, by J.I. Biegelsen (New York: Grosset and Dunlap, 1976). How to write résumés, how to present them, and how to prepare for an interview. Alphabetical list of sample résumés from accountant to x-ray technician, with many applicable to religious careers.

What Color Is Your Parachute? by Richard Nelson Bolles (Berkeley: Ten Speed Press, 1978). Concentrates on changing careers, but is helpful to anyone. Special section on help for the clergy and religious.

Where Do I Go from Here with My Life, by John C. Crystal and Richard N. Bolles (New York: Seabury Press, 1974). A work manual to accompany *What Color Is Your Parachute?*

Working Loose, by New Vocations Project of the American Friends Service Committee (New York: Random House, 1972). A series of readings about finding satisfying work. Describes the experiences of individuals who developed alternative careers.

Index of Careers

For other listings of individual careers, see also:
1. The complete list of Christian work opportunities beginning on page 121.
2. Appendix A: "A Listing of Church Occupations," page 217

247

Index of Churches, Organizations, Groups, and Companies

For additional listings see also:
1. "Denominational Career Offices," Appendix C, page 234
2. "Church Career Development Centers," Appendix D, page 237

249